VOLUME 7

D1414817

FIRST and SECOND CHRONICLES

Leonard T. Wolcott

ABINGDON PRESS
Nashville

1 and 2 Chronicles

Copyright © 1988 by Graded Press

This book is printed on recycled, acid-free paper.

Library of Congress Cataloging-in-Publication Data

Cokesbury basic Bible commentary.
  Basic Bible commentary / by Linda B. Hinton . . . [et.al.].
    p.   cm.
  Originally published: Cokesbury basic Bible commentary. Nashville: Graded Press, © 1988.
  ISBN 0-687-02620-2 (pbk. : v. 1 : alk. paper)
  1. Bible—Commentaries. I. Hinton, Linda B. II. Title.
[BS491.2.C65   1994]
220.7—dc20   94-10965
                                                                            CIP

ISBN 0-687-02626-1 (v. 7, 1–2 Chronicles)
ISBN 0-687-02620-2 (v. 1, Genesis)
ISBN 0-687-02621-0 (v. 2, Exodus–Leviticus)
ISBN 0-687-02622-9 (v. 3, Numbers–Deuteronomy)
ISBN 0-687-02623-7 (v. 4, Joshua–Ruth)
ISBN 0-687-02624-5 (v. 5, 1–2 Samuel)
ISBN 0-687-02625-3 (v. 6, 1–2 Kings)
ISBN 0-687-02627-X (v. 8, Ezra–Esther)
ISBN 0-687-02628-8 (v. 9, Job)
ISBN 0-687-02629-6 (v. 10, Psalms)
ISBN 0-687-02630-X (v. 11, Proverbs–Song of Solomon)
ISBN 0-687-02631-8 (v. 12, Isaiah)
ISBN 0-687-02632-6 (v. 13, Jeremiah–Lamentations)
ISBN 0-687-02633-4 (v. 14, Ezekiel–Daniel)
ISBN 0-687-02634-2 (v. 15, Hosea–Jonah)
ISBN 0-687-02635-0 (v. 16, Micah–Malachi)
ISBN 0-687-02636-9 (v. 17, Matthew)
ISBN 0-687-02637-7 (v. 18, Mark)
ISBN 0-687-02638-5 (v. 19, Luke)
ISBN 0-687-02639-3 (v. 20, John)
ISBN 0-687-02640-7 (v. 21, Acts)
ISBN 0-687-02642-3 (v. 22, Romans)
ISBN 0-687-02643-1 (v. 23, 1–2 Corinthians)
ISBN 0-687-02644-X (v. 24, Galatians–Ephesians)
ISBN 0-687-02645-8 (v. 25, Philippians–2 Thessalonians)
ISBN 0-687-02646-6 (v. 26, 1 Timothy–Philemon)
ISBN 0-687-02647-4 (v. 27, Hebrews)
ISBN 0-687-02648-2 (v. 28, James–Jude)
ISBN 0-687-02649-0 (v. 29, Revelation)
ISBN 0-687-02650-4 (complete set of 29 vols.)

01 02 03—10 9 8 7 6 5 4 3 2

MANUFACTURED IN THE UNITED STATES OF AMERICA

Contents

Outline of 1 and 2 Chronicles. 4
Introduction to 1 and 2 Chronicles 7

1. 1 Chronicles 1–5 11
2. 1 Chronicles 6:1–9:34 20
3. 1 Chronicles 9:35–12:40 28
4. 1 Chronicles 13–20 37
5. 1 Chronicles 21:1–23:1 46
6. 1 Chronicles 23:2–26:32 53
7. 1 Chronicles 27–29 59
8. 2 Chronicles 1:1–5:1 67
9. 2 Chronicles 5–7 73
10. 2 Chronicles 8–9. 79
11. 2 Chronicles 10–13 87
12. 2 Chronicles 14–16 95
13. 2 Chronicles 17–20 103
14. 2 Chronicles 21–24 111
15. 2 Chronicles 25–28 121
16. 2 Chronicles 29–32 130
17. 2 Chronicles 33–36 138

Glossary of Terms 146
Guide to Pronunciation 153
Map of the Kingdom
    of David and Solomon. 158
Map of the Kingdoms of
    Israel and Judah. 159
Map of the Ancient Near East. 160

Outline

First Chronicles

I. From Adam to Jacob (1:1-34)
II. The Descendants of Esau (1:35-54)
III. The Descendants of Jacob (2:1–8:40)
    A. The sons of Israel (2:1-2)
    B. Descendants of Judah and Simeon (2:3–4:43)
    C. Descendants of Reuben and Gad (5:1-17)
    D. The eastern Israelites (5:18-26)
    E. The family of Levi (6:1-81)
    F. Descendants of Issachar and Benjamin (7:1-12)
    G. Descendants of Naphtali and Manasseh (7:13-19)
    H. The family of Ephraim (7:20-29)
    I. The descendants of Asher (7:30-40)
    J. The family of Benjamin (8:1-40)
IV. The Exile and After (9:1-34)
V. King Saul (9:35–10:14)
VI. David's Kingship (11:1–12:40)
    A. The choice of all Israel (11:1-3)
    B. David's capture of Jerusalem (11:4-9)
    C. David's warriors (11:10-47)
    D. David's supporters (12:1-22)
    E. David's coronation at Hebron (12:23-40)
VII. David and the Ark of the Covenant (13:1–17:27)
    A. Bringing the ark from Kiriath-jearim (13:1-14)
    B. David's house and home (14:1-7)

      C. Victories over the Philistines (14:8-15)
      D. The ark of God in Zion (15:1–16:43)
      E. David's desire to build a temple (17:1-15)
      F. David's prayer (17:16-27)
VIII. The House of David (18:1–20:8)
      A. David's conquests (18:1-13)
      B. David's government (18:14-17)
      C. Campaign against the Ammonites (19:1–20:3)
      D. Heroes against the Philistines (20:4-8)
  IX. The Military Census (21:1–22:1)
   X. David and the House of the Lord (22:2–26:32)
      A. Preparing for the temple of the Lord (22:2–23:1)
      B. Organization of priests and Levites (23:2–26:32)
  XI. David's Administration (27:1-34)
 XII. David's Final Arrangements (28:1–29:25)
XIII. David's Death (29:26-30)

Second Chronicles

   I. The Building of the Temple (1:1–7:22)
      A. Solomon's reign initiated with worship (1:1-6)
      B. Solomon's worship and God's presence (1:7-13)
      C. God's blessings on Solomon (1:14-17)
      D. Preparations to build the Temple (2:1–3:2)
      E. Temple measurements and description (3:3–5:1)
      F. The Temple finished (5:1)
      G. The ark of the covenant to the Temple (5:1–6:1)
      H. Solomon's prayer of dedication (6:2-42)
      I. The closing ceremonies (7:1-11)
      J. God's reply to Solomon's prayer (7:12-22)
  II. The Greatness of Solomon (8:1–9:31)
 III. The Division of the Kingdom (10:1–11:4)
      A. Rehoboam's response to the people (10:1-15)
      B. Separation of the northern tribes (10:16-19)
      C. Failure to quell the rebellion (11:1-4)
 IV. The Reign of Rehoboam (11:5–12:16)
  V. The Reign of Abijah (13:1-22)

VI. The Reign of Asa (14:1–16:14)
VII. The Reign of Jehoshaphat (17:1–20:37)
    A. Jehoshaphat's piety and prosperity (17:1-6)
    B. Jehoshaphat, the religious educator (17:7-9)
    C. Jehoshaphat's greatness (17:10-19)
    D. Jehoshaphat's alliance with Ahab (18:1–19:3)
    E. Jehoshaphat's judicial system (19:4-11)
    F. Jehoshaphat's victory (20:1-30)
    G. Jehoshaphat's last days (20:31-34)
    H. The wreck of merchant ships (20:35-37)
VIII. Jehoram's Reign (21:1-20)
IX. Ahaziah's Reign (22:1-9)
X. Athaliah Reigns; Jehoiada Revolts (22:10–23:21)
    A. Prince Joash hidden from Athaliah (22:10-12)
    B. Conspiracy and covenant (23:1-21)
XI. The Reign of Joash (24:1-27)
XII. The Reign of Amaziah (25:1-28)
XIII. The Reign of Uzziah (26:1-23)
XIV. The Reign of Jotham (27:1-9)
XV. The Reign of Ahaz (28:1-27)
XVI. The Reign of Hezekiah (29:1–32:33)
    A. Restoration of Temple worship (29:1-36)
    B. The renewal of Israel (30:1-27)
    C. Renewal of right religious practices (31:1-21)
    D. The threat from Assyria (32:1-23)
    E. The close of Hezekiah's reign (32:24-33)
XVII. Manasseh and Amon (33:1-25)
XVIII. The Reign of Josiah (34:1–35:27)
    A. Josiah's faithfulness (34:1-33)
    B. Josiah's celebration of the Passover (35:1-19)
    C. The death of Josiah (35:20-27)
XIX. The Last of the Kings of Judah (36:1-21)
    A. Jehoahaz and Egypt (36:1-4)
    B. Jehoiakim, Jehoiachin, and Babylon (36:5-10)
    C. Zedekiah's and Judah's unfaithfulness (36:11-16)
    D. Destruction and exile of the people (36:17-21)
XX. Cyrus of Persia: Hope for Jerusalem (36:22-23)

1 AND 2 CHRONICLES

Introduction to 1 and 2 Chronicles

The Hebrew title is "Events of the Days," that is, "Chronicles." The Hebrews put Chronicles at the end of their Bible because it was a later addition to all that had been said and written.

Following written histories and records of his people, the writer of Chronicles recast them with the fresh viewpoint and attitudes that experience had brought to Israel. He applied them to the needs of his times and of all times.

The Historical Period Covered

The Chronicles cover the period of Judah's history as a kingdom. First, however, the books trace the background of world history from Adam to Jacob, the ancestor of Israel. They trace Jacob's descendants to the end of the reign of Israel's first king, Saul. The main story of Chronicles begins with the reign of David, 1000 B.C., and continues to the last king, Zedekiah, and the fall of Jerusalem, 586 B.C. During these more than 400 years, the world political powers were Egypt, to the south of Judah; and Assyria, in the north, until 625 B.C. when Babylonia, to the east, replaced Assyria as a world power.

Chronicles' Interpretation of History

The Chronicler wrote his book with the conviction that God is the creator and controller of nature, and the ruler over history. History, under God, is a matter of divine selection and of development by divine revelation.

Through the generations, God prepared for and selected Israel as the chosen people. Of all Israel, God chose the tribe of Judah to be its leader (1 Chronicles 28:4). And in all Judah, God chose Jerusalem (2 Chronicles 6:6). From the descendants of Israel God chose David and his heirs to rule the people. God chose David's son, Solomon, to build a temple: *The house of the Lord*. Chronicles is a history of the Temple.

Chronicles records the history of the kings of David's dynasty and of the people of Israel in relation to the Temple and what it represents: God's rule and presence and purpose, the law and commandments, God's covenant with, and compassion for, the chosen people (and always the power of God's righteousness). For Chronicles, all that happened before Moses was pre-history. Moses, followed by Joshua, established Israel as a theocracy, a God-ruled people. The period of David followed by Solomon, who duplicated Moses and Joshua, was the fulfillment of God's kingdom on earth. The kings in David's line were God's stewards. When they were faithful, God blessed them. When they were unfaithful, God punished them. If they repented and returned to God, they were pardoned.

The Chronicler's Purpose

The Chronicler writes to inform his readers, through the story of their nation, how God's judgment works. He writes to urge them to be faithful worshipers at the Temple, to keep the covenant, the law and commandments, and to *do what is right in the eyes of the Lord*. He writes to warn them that what happened to their ancestors and to their nation as the result of faithlessness can happen again to them. He also writes to encourage them that, despite the Exile and the loss of their kingdom and David's dynasty of kings, there is yet hope for them. The people can sincerely hope for a renewal of those good days through faithfulness to God, who is faithful to them in return.

Date

The date of composition of Chronicles is, as the work itself states, after the return from exile (537 B.C.). First Chronicles mentions money coined not before 515 B.C. (1 Chronicles 29:7). It takes David's lineage to the sixth generation after Zerubbabel, who was governor of Jerusalem under Darius at the end of the sixth century B.C. (1 Chronicles 3:19-24). Scholars believe that Chronicles was written after Ezra-Nehemiah was written (as one book), but the book of Nehemiah records the high priests down to Jaddua, who was high priest at the time of Alexander of Macedonia (late fourth century B.C.). Jaddua expressed goals and a zeal similar to those of the Chronicles, which uses the late Hebrew of that century. All this evidence indicates that the Chronicler wrote his work shortly after 350 B.C.

Author

The author does not name himself. Like Ezra-Nehemiah, Chronicles has a structure and a theology that emphasize counsel, covenant-making, purification of the land and people, and renewal of the Temple ritual. This similarity is due to its author belonging to the same community and epoch. Nevertheless, there are marked differences in vocabulary and in attitudes toward non-Jews. The Chronicler places a strong emphasis, lacking in Ezra-Nehemiah, on the Levites, their importance and tasks. Because the author writes in Levitical preaching style, and because he speaks more highly of the Levites than of the priests, many have thought the author may have been a Levite. The special place he gives to music among the Levites may mean he was also a musician.

One Book

Chronicles is one book with four sections: (1) the introduction, the genealogies (1 Chronicles 1–9); (2) the story of King David and plans for the Temple (1 Chronicles 10–29); (3) the story of King Solomon and the building of the Temple (2 Chronicles 1–9); and (4) the stories of the kings of Judah (2 Chronicles 10–36). The book was divided into 1 and 2 Chronicles simply because it was too long to go on one papyrus roll; each half fit neatly on one roll.

Sources

The Chronicler refers to a variety of sourcebooks about the kings of Israel and of Judah, including 1 and 2 Samuel and 1 and 2 Kings. About half of the Chronicles' verses are quoted from them. The phrase *parallel to* in this commentary refers to passages that are copies verbatim or are partly quoted, or are on the same subject but written differently. References to books of seers and prophets are to their appearances in Samuel and Kings (or, in one instance, in Isaiah). There being no division by chapters and books, the sections of a book were referred to by the persons storied in them, just as Paul, in Romans 11:2, refers to what was written *in Elijah* (the Greek is *in*, not *of*) when he refers to 1 Kings 19. Genealogies from Genesis through 2 Kings are used, as well as military records and censuses, lists of Levites and of prominent families, local and family records and reminiscences, and oral tradition. The author uses the Psalms freely and phrases from the prophets. It is probable that some additions have been made by a later editor. This seems to be the case when references about priests are added that do not quite fit the text.

Introduction to These Chapters

Beginning with Adam, Chronicles follows a selective genealogy of those lines that lead down to Jacob, renamed Israel. Then the Chronicler takes the sons of Jacob and their genealogies. Jacob's sons (except, in place of Joseph, Joseph's two sons) are the tribes of Israel, and Chronicles traces the genealogy of each. The list begins with Judah and then moves to Simeon which, the only tribe south of Judah, became absorbed into Judah. It then traces the tribes who were allocated land east of the Dead Sea and of the Jordan River: Reuben, Gad, and the eastern part of Manasseh.

Here is an outline of these chapters.
I. From Adam to Jacob (1:1-34)
II. The Descendants of Esau (1:35-54)
III. The Sons of Israel (2:1-2)
IV. The Lineage of Judah (2:3-55)
V. The Line of David (3:1-24)
   A. The family of David (3:1-9)
   B. The kings of Judah (3:10-15)
   C. The royal descendants without a throne (3:16-24)
VI. More Descendants of Judah (4:1-23)
VII. The Descendants of Simeon (4:24-43)
VIII. The Descendants of Reuben (5:1-10)
IX. The Descendants of Gad (5:11-17)
X. The Eastern Israelites (5:18-22)
XI. The Eastern Half of Manasseh (5:23-26)

From Adam to Jacob (1:1-34)

Verses 1-4 list the names recorded in Genesis 5 from *Adam* to *Noah*, finishing with the sons of Noah. Noah's son, Shem, whose name is given first, is the ancestor claimed by the people of Israel. The Chronicler traces first the lineage of *Japheth* (verses 5-7) and then that of *Ham* (verses 8-16) before returning to Shem's line in verse 17. Chronicles simply copies the list of names in Genesis 10, omitting the geographical and historical references that are irrelevant to this history. There are occasional mistakes in the text, such as *Diphath* for the original *Riphath* (verse 6), and *Rodanim* for *Dodanim* (verse 7).

The Chronicler fails to include *sons of* after Noah (verse 4) and after *Aram* (verse 17), whose sons were *Uz, Hul, Gether and Meshech* (see Genesis 10:23). He selects the names (verses 24-27) that are in the direct line to Abraham, copied from Genesis 11:10-26. *Abram*'s name (verse 27) was changed to *Abraham* on the basis of his faith (see Genesis 17:5).

Ishmael is mentioned along with Isaac in verse 28 because he was borne on behalf of Sarah by her maid, Hagar. Verses 28-33 list descendants of Abraham's other sons. Sons of Abraham by his concubine, Keturah, are considered of less importance, although her descendants are added after Ishmael's (verses 32-33). As in the case of Noah's descendants (verses 5-16), they are listed before Chronicles returns to the line that will lead to Israel. Verses 29-31 are copied from Genesis 25:13-16. Verses 32-33 are taken from Genesis 25:1-4.

The Descendants of Esau (1:35-54)

Of the sons of Isaac, Esau and Jacob, Chronicles first lists *the sons of Esau*. As with the children of Noah (verses 5-24) and of Abraham (verses 28-33), Chronicles lists first the line that is not of Israel's ancestry. This list (verses 35-37) is taken from Genesis 36:4-5, 10-14. A reference to Genesis 36:12 makes clear that *Timna* (a woman's name) was not a son but was the concubine of Eliphaz. She was *the sister* of Lotan (verse 39). Her son was Amalek.

In verses 38-42 the sons and grandsons of *Seir* are listed. Seir may have been the name of a clan *in the hill country of Seir* (Genesis 36:8) in Edom, where Esau is said to have settled (Genesis 36:19).

In verses 43-54 the Chronicler compresses the list of the kings and chiefs of Edom in Genesis 36:31-43.

The Sons of Israel (2:1-2)

Isaac's two sons were *Esau and Israel* (1:34). In Genesis 32:28, Jacob's name was changed to Israel, *for you have striven with God and with humans, and have prevailed* (NRSV). In the NIV, the explanation is phrased in this way: *because you have struggled with God and with men and have overcome.* From this the people of Israel derive their name. Israel (Jacob) had twelve sons. They were all ancestors of the nation of Israel. In this way the Chronicler presses the point that Israel is not just Judah, but is all twelve tribes.

The next eight chapters give the lineage of the twelve, minus two: Zebulun and Dan are missing. Perhaps a small portion of the Chronicler's account, including these two tribes, was lost at an early date. The list of the twelve sons follows Genesis 35:23-26, except that *Dan* is listed as the seventh, before Rachel's sons, *Joseph* and *Benjamin.* Dan was borne before them by Bilhah, Rachel's maid, on her behalf (Genesis 30:1-6).

The Chronicles lists of the descendants of Israel's sons have been drawn from several sources, both biblical (Genesis 46; Numbers 26) and non-biblical (such as family and census records).

The Lineage of Judah (2:3-55)

The descendants of *Judah* are given first and greater attention because Judah has preeminence as the ancestor of David, Israel's glorious king (see 5:2). The story of

Judah's sons (verses 3-4) is taken from Genesis 38. *Tamar*, Judah's daughter-in-law and a non-Jew, became, by Judah's illicit sexual act with her (Leviticus 18:15; 20:12), the ancestress of David (and of Jesus: Matthew 1:3). The Chronicler calls attention to non-Israelites in his genealogies in the face of racial purists among his contemporaries. Verses 6-8 list descendants of *Zerah* before going on to his brother, *Perez*, who was ancestor to David. Zerah's descendants: *Ethan, Heman, Calcol and Dara* (verse 6) are mentioned as wise men in 1 Kings 4:31, and as Ezrahites in the headings of Psalms 88 and 89. *Achar's* story is from Joshua 7:16-26, where he is called *Achan*. Achar, in Hebrew, means *to trouble, to bring bad luck. Chelubai (Caleb)* in verse 9 is the same Caleb of verse 18.

Beginning with verse 9 and continuing through 3:24, the Chronicler records the family of *Hezron*—also found in Ruth 4:19-22—from which line came the kings of Judah. The family of *Ram* (2:10-17) includes *Jesse* and his sons, of whom David was the seventh. According to 1 Samuel 16:6-13, David is the eighth son. Seven is a more sacred number. *Zeruiah* and *Abigail* (verse 16) are called David's sisters, which means they were closely related, not necessarily siblings of the same parents. They are called daughters of Nahash (not Jesse) in 2 Samuel 17:25. *Amasa* was the son of Abigail, who was married to a non-Israelite (verse 17).

Chronicles returns to the family of Ram's brother, Caleb (2:18-24). The author has pieced this story together from different sources (see verse 24 below), and it is not well organized. This is not the Caleb sent as a spy into Canaan (Numbers 13:6), who belongs to a later generation. The family list ends with *Bezalel* (verse 20), whose importance is that he is identified with the builder of the tabernacle in Exodus (31:2; 35:30). The *sixty towns* belonged to a kingdom to the north of Israel near Damascus.

The descendants of *Jerahmeel* (2:25-33), Hezron's oldest

son, are a clan living in the southern part of Judah in an area known as the Negeb (1 Samuel 27:10; 30:29). More details are added about the family of Jerahmeel (2:34-41). *Jarha* was an *Egyptian servant (slave)* brought into a Jewish family.

The Calebites (2:42-55) are referred to as a clan in 1 Samuel 25. Several of the names in this list can be identified as names of places near and beyond *Hebron*, south of Jerusalem. Hebron was, according to Joshua 14:13, given to Caleb. The descendants of *Hur* (2:50-55), son of Caleb by his second wife (verse 19), include place names of clans in the area of *Kiriath-jearim* near Jerusalem.

The Family of David (3:1-9)

Hebron was David's first capital (2 Samuel 5:5). For similar lists of David's sons born in *Hebron*, see 2 Samuel 3:2-5, and born in *Jerusalem*, see 2 Samuel 5:14-16.

The Kings of Judah (3:10-15)

Judah's kings were descendants of David through *Solomon*. *Azariah* is Uzziah of 2 Chronicles 26 (and 2 Kings 15:13, 34; Isaiah 1:1; 6:1). *Shallum, Josiah's* son, is Jehoahaz (2 Kings 23:30 and 2 Chronicles 36:1). Jeremiah calls him king (Jeremiah 22:11).

The Royal Descendants Without a Throne (3:16-24)

Johanan and *Zedekiah*, descendants of Jehoiakim, were not kings. *Jeconiah*, found in verse 16 of the NRSV, is the same *Jehoiachin* of 2 Kings 24:8 and is translated accordingly in the NIV.

The list of David's descendants, after Judah fell to the Chaldean empire and were carried off into exile in Babylon (586 B.C.), is carried down to the time of the Chronicler. *Zerubbabel* is the more prominent among them, and his family is better known, because he was a leader in bringing exiles back to Jerusalem. Cyrus, the Persian conqueror of Babylon, allowed and encouraged their return (Ezra 1:1-4; 2:1-2). Zerubbabel's children's names are listed. The names spell words and phrases indicative of the renewed zeal of the returning exiles, a zeal stressed by the Chronicler: *Meshullam—the regenerated people of Israel; Hananiah—God extends lovingkindness; Jushab-hesed—the people have returned to Judah because of God's love. Ohel* means *tent,* like the tent of meeting that the exiles set up where the destroyed Temple had stood.

More Descendants of Judah (4:1-23)

The Chronicler returns to the descendants of Judah at the point where he interrupted his list to enlarge on David's line. This list differs from the list beginning with 2:3. Scholars have suggested that a later editor may have added this list. In the middle of the genealogy comes an interesting story about *Jabez* (verse 10). His is the first of many prayers quoted by the Chronicler, for whom prayer is a vital element in the life of God's obedient people.

The sons of Kenaz . . . The sons of Caleb (verses 13-15): The spy Caleb is called a Kenizzite in Numbers 32:12; Joshua 14:6, 14. The Kenizzites are thought to be a southern clan that was identified with Judah. Another non-Jew, the daughter of Pharaoh (verse 17), joins the list. *Shelah* (verse 21) is the last son of Judah.

Linen-workers and *potters* suggest that families were identified by the trade or craft that they followed. With the note that the records are ancient, the Chronicler closes his list of the line of Judah.

The Descendants of Simeon (4:24-43)

Simeon, historically and geographically, was a tribe closely linked with Judah (Joshua 19:1, 9; Judges 1:3). The listing of Simeonite towns (4:28-33) is taken from Joshua 19:2-8. *These were their towns until David reigned* (verse 31). South of Judah, in the Negeb, they were absorbed into Judah. Population pressure on the land forced the

Simeonites to push outward for more pasture into *Gedor* (verse 39) and westward into Philistine land (see 2 Kings 18:8). *Meunim (Meunites)* were people from Ma'an, south of the Dead Sea. The word, however, may be confused with *dwelling places* in Hebrew. Another southward push toward Mount Seir is recorded in verses 42-43.

The Descendants of Reuben (5:1-10)

The eldest son of Jacob was *Reuben*. His descendants are traced in a manner similar to Simeon's. To explain why Reuben's line is treated later and less fully than Judah's, the Chronicler makes clear that Reuben forfeited his birthright as eldest son. He lost it when he slept with Bilhah, his father's concubine (Genesis 35:22; see also Genesis 49:4). A more important reason for the Chronicler is, however, that Judah became a stronger, more aggressive tribe and that *a ruler* (David) came from Judah. Reuben's blessing was given by his father to the sons of Joseph, Manasseh and Ephraim, whose descendants became the core of northern Israel.

The Reuben genealogy is taken from Numbers 26:5-9. The account of the Assyrian emperor, *Tilgath-pilneser* (Tiglath-pileser), grasping from Israel part of her northern border states, is told in 2 Kings 15:29. Verses 8-10 tell where Reuben's descendants lived, following Numbers 32:38 and Joshua 13:15-23. This was the hilly country east of the Dead Sea. Verses 9 and 10 suggest that they spread eastward and northward. *Hagrites* were one of the tribes that are described in the section "The Eastern Israelites (5:18-22)."

The Descendants of Gad (5:11-17)

The phrasing of this section, in its similarity to that of the Reuben list, suggests not only that the Chronicler had a common source, a list made during the reign of Jotham king of Judah (verse 17), but also that there was a common culture and a mingling of these tribes. *The sons of Gad (Gadites)* lived next to the Reubenites, having been allotted land just to the north, east of the Jordan (verse 11). The land of Gad is commonly called *Gilead* (verse 14). *Bashan*, which means *fertile land*, was situated just northeast of Gilead (verses 11, 12, 16). No *pasture lands of Sharon* east of the Jordan are known. *Upland pasture* may be the meaning.

The Eastern Israelites (5:18-22)

On the east side of the Dead Sea and Jordan River, two and a half tribes were supposed to be located: Reuben, Gad, and half of *Manasseh*. They were cut off from the east by desert and were never free possessors of the land, which was also claimed by non-Israelite tribes and kingdoms. This gave them need for a common defense. The tribes mentioned here (verse 19) were tribes that, like so many before and since, were pushing in from the Arabian desert. In verses 20 and 22, for the first of many times, the Chronicler makes the point that battles are won for people who trust in and obey God, not by their might, but by God's power. The figures in verse 21 are the first among many inflated figures in Chronicles. *Until the exile* (verse 22) means until they were forcibly removed by the Assyrian king, Tiglath-pileser, in 734 B.C. (verse 26).

The Eastern Half of Manasseh (5:23-26)

The tribe of Manasseh was a large one, spread through northern Israel on both sides of the Jordan. According to verse 23, the eastern group reached from Bashan, north of Gilead (which was just to the south of the sea of Galilee), all the way north to the mountain range of which Mount Hermon was the southern peak and from which flowed the waters that eventually became the Jordan River and the Dead Sea. More space is given to this tribe in 7:14-19. The list here is from a military census, as it mentions *heads of their clans (families)* and *mighty (brave) warriors*.

Verses 25-26 belong with the previous remarks (verses 18-20) about all the eastern tribes of Israel. The emphasis contrasts with that of verses 20-22, that God helps those who obey. Chronicles repeats throughout that, when people transgress against God's laws and are disloyal to God, God brings trouble to them. The story here is based on the account in 2 Kings 15:19, 29; 17:6-23; 18:11.

Pul and *Tilgath-pilneser* are two names for the same king: Tiglath-pileser. The land to which the eastern tribes were exiled, *Gozan*, was actually a city and district on the *Habor* River, north and east of the Euphrates River.

§ § § § § § §

The Message of 1 Chronicles 1–5

God is in charge of the creation. Down through the generations, persons are selected to carry out God's purpose. Most people in each generation are only names when they are gone. Some achieve fame for a time, but it is lost. Some violate the rules that society makes. Some are considered "outsiders." But God uses generation after generation to build toward the goal of a people of God's own choosing, and toward a splendor among those who obey God's law and trust in God.

Whatever may have happened to all the descendants of Adam, it was his descendant Jacob, called Israel, whom God found acceptable to be the ancestor of the chosen people. All Israel's descendants and all those who were brought into relationship with them were God's people. Among them, God chose David to set up a society that would be the ideal society. Whatever David's descendants were like in the royal line of kings, each had the potential of maintaining a God-obeying and God-trusting society.

Each of us, in our time, has the potential of receiving the way of God and passing it on to the next generation.

§ § § § § § §

1 Chronicles 6:1–9:34

Introduction to These Chapters

Here the Chronicler's attention is on the Levites, who were the caretakers of Israel's religious life. Special attention is given to the Levites who were priests and to those who were singers at worship services. Space is also given to their distribution among the various tribes of Israel.

Then follow genealogies of the six tribes who made up the main body of northern Israel. The last list is of the tribe of Benjamin, which furnished Israel with its first king, with whose family the genealogical lists end.

The genealogies are carried down to a period in history when the inhabitants of Jerusalem, having been exiled by the Chaldean conqueror Nebuchadnezzar, were allowed to return by the Persian emperor, Cyrus. Therefore, the Chronicler lists by families the citizens who had returned to Jerusalem from exile.

Here is an outline of these chapters.
  I. The Family of Levi (6:1-81)
 II. The Descendants of Issachar (7:1-5)
III. The Descendants of Benjamin (7:6-12)
 IV. The Descendants of Naphtali (7:13)
  V. The Descendants of Manasseh (7:14-19)
 VI. The Family of Ephraim (7:20-29)
VII. The Descendants of Asher (7:30-40)
VIII. The Family of Benjamin (8:1-40)
 IX. The Exile and After (9:1-34)

The Family of Levi (6:1-81)

Moses, who led Israel to freedom from Egypt, and his brother, *Aaron,* the first high priest of Israel, belonged to this tribe. Instead of being given their own part of Canaan to settle in, the Levites were distributed in towns and cities throughout Israel so as to serve all other tribes as priests (the descendants of Aaron) and as priests' assistants (all Levites of other than Aaron's family). Because the central purpose of Chronicles is to record the history of worship at the Temple, special attention is given to the Levites throughout the book. As priests and officers of the religious life of Israel, their genealogical records may have been available to the Chronicler in greater completeness than those of most tribes. The author, himself probably a Levite, symbolically placed the list of Levites at the center of his lists.

Chronicles breaks down the list of Levites by family branch, by kind of service performed, and by the sections of Israel where they were appointed to live. The *Levites* traced their family through three main branches: those of *Gershom, Kohath,* and *Merari.*

First of all, Chronicles reports on the foremost of the Levite descendants, the high priest who belonged to the Kohath line. The line begins with *Aaron,* the first high priest; his brother, *Moses;* and their sister, *Miriam.* The Chronicler selects the line of Aaron's descendants, who, according to the author, became high priests in succession. The list continues until the *exile.*

The Chronicler lists again the three sons of Levi, and the sons of each of them (verses 16-19). The Gershom line is extended in verses 20-21, the Kohath line in verses 22-27, and the Merari line in verses 29-30. (Another list of names of Levite descendants appears in Exodus 6:16-25.) Verse 28 adds the name of *Samuel* and his two sons without indicating if and how they are related to the Levi descendants (compare 1 Samuel 8:2).

Verses 31-48 list the singers, appointed by David, and

their Levite ancestors. Just as the listing of the Levites is central in the genealogical lists of the tribes of Israel, so the listing of Levite singers is central in the lists of Levites because worship, which the singers lead, is central in the Chronicler's image of Israel.

The Chronicler attributes their establishment to *David*. David's reputation as a musician and psalmist goes back to the kingdom's earliest traditions and records (1 Samuel 19:9; 2 Samuel 6:5; 23:1). All the best in Israel's history and religion will be attributed by Chronicles to David's reign. These Levites were appointed by David for the celebration of the ark that will be narrated in 15:26-28.

The genealogy of musicians is given in reverse order. Beginning with *Heman* (here listed as the grandson of Samuel) and *Asaph* and *Ethan,* the lines are traced back to the forefathers of each of the three branches of the Levi tribe. These lists may come from records kept by the Levite musicians. Several psalms are attributed to the family music guilds set up by each of these singers. Verse 48 underlines a point that Chronicles keeps before the readers: the rightful place of Levites, not only of priests, in Temple worship.

Verses 49-53 trace the direct descendants of *Aaron*. Distinct from the ministries of other Levites, they served as priests; and to the descendants of his grandson, Phinehas, was reserved the high priesthood. Verse 49 describes their duties in line with those described in the book of Leviticus (as in Leviticus 1:3-9).

Finally, the Levite settlements are listed in verses 54-81 (as copied from Joshua 21:5-39). Instead of settling in one section of Canaan as the other tribes did, the Levites were dispersed throughout Israel. In his review, the Chronicler makes evident to the reader not only the extent of David's kingdom but also the unity of faith and worship that the Levite settlements signify. The record begins with the Kohath branch of Levites, first with the descendants of Aaron (verses 54-65) and then the rest of the families of the Kohathites (verses 66-70). Then follow the Gershom branch (verses 71-76) and the Merari branch (verses 77-81). *Their settlement locations* include towns and cities and surrounding pasture lands.

The cities of refuge (verses 57, 67) were six selected cities in six parts of Israel to which anyone who killed another unintentionally might flee for sanctuary, where he would be protected from vengeance until he could be given a fair trial (Numbers 35:9-15). All six cities would be for Levites, besides forty-two towns with surrounding pastureland as described in Numbers 35:1-8.

The Descendants of Issachar (7:1-5)

With a basis in Numbers 26:23-25, this list comes from a military census with its reference to warriors and chiefs. Probably records were few in the smaller tribes.

The Descendants of Benjamin (7:6-12)

Like the previous list, this one seems to be drawn from a census, used for military purposes, of effective soldiers and commanders.

The Descendants of Naphtali (7:13)

This list corresponds to Genesis 46:24, and is very brief. The genealogies of the tribes of Dan and Zebulun, sons of Jacob, are altogether missing. Some scholars have suggested that they were lost, or not available to the author, or mixed by mistake in other lists: for example, that of Benjamin in verses 6-12.

The Descendants of Manasseh (7:14-19)

A military census has already been used in a brief notice of the family of eastern Manasseh, east of the Jordan (5:24). This genealogy of the tribe of *Manasseh* is similar to the list found in Numbers 26:29-34 and Joshua

17. The tribe of Manasseh is associated with a large extent of the area that came to be northern Israel.

The Family of Ephraim (7:20-29)

This list (compare Numbers 26:35-36, from which it differs) includes the famed *Joshua*, son of Nun, leader of Israel after Moses (verse 27; see Joshua 1:1-2). This section of the genealogy includes two interesting stories that were probably in the Ephraim family tradition. They come out of Ephraim's pioneer days. Ephraim settlers located, along with the tribe of Dan, south of Manasseh and north of the border of Judah. In the southwestern part of Ephraim, the land extends into an area claimed by the Philistines. *Gath* (verse 21) is not to be confused with the Philistine city of Gath farther south.

The story in verses 21-22 refers to the push westward, clashing with native residents (verse 21). The pathos in verse 22 is unusual in the genealogical lists. The story in verse 24 refers to towns in the same area, slightly to the east. *Bethel* and *Shechem* became prominent cities in the nation of Israel. *Megiddo* was far to the north in the Plain of Esdraelon, fertile passageway for invading armies and, therefore, a frequent battleground. Megiddo and Shechem were located in the area that was supposed to belong to the tribe of Manasseh. Manasseh and Ephraim were not of the twelve sons of Jacob, but were his grandsons, sons of Joseph (verse 29; see Genesis 48:5-6, 13-14). They completed the twelve tribal sections, since the Levites never became a geographically distinct tribe.

The Descendants of Asher (7:30-40)

This list is taken from a military census (verse 40; compare Genesis 46:17 and Numbers 26:44-47).

The Family of Benjamin (8:1-40)

This chapter is the last of the tribal genealogies. It is the longest except for Judah and Levi. *Benjamin* was an integral part of the Southern Kingdom, Judah, and more lists may, therefore, have been available to the author. There seem to be several lists for different periods and locations. These lists vary in the names given for the sons of Benjamin. But the word *sons* does not necessarily refer to immediate children; it can mean prominent clan leaders in the line of descent from Benjamin.

The list previously recorded (7:6-12) may be a late list from a period after the return of Israel from exile. Benjaminites *of Geba* (8:1-7) lived in hill country. The reference to exile is not clear. The Hebrew words allow the suggestion that Geba's previous inhabitants were driven out and withdrew south to *Manahath* in Judah.

There were Benjaminites in *Moab* (8:8-11). This colony of Benjamin must have settled there shortly after other tribal groups had arrived in Canaan. Moab was east of the Dead Sea.

Verse 12 seems to connect the following list with the previous one (verses 8-11). *Ono* and *Lod* were ancient towns in the Valley of Aijalon, which slopes to the Mediterranean Sea near Joppa. The city of *Aijalon* at the valley head would mean an extension of Benjaminites westward from their original settlement (8:12-27). This is near the town of Gath (verse 13) mentioned in 7:21.

Clans of Benjaminites lived in Jerusalem (8:28), which was on the border of Benjamin. It is not clear where the list of those who lived in Jerusalem begins.

The final list is of the house of Saul (8:29-40), a family branch who lived in the area of *Gibeon*. If this record is correct, *Saul*, the first king of Israel, belonged to this branch. The list is much different, however, from the ancestor list for Saul found in 1 Samuel 9:1. The first names on this list may go back to the early settlement of the tribe. At some time in their history, part of the tribe moved to the big city of Jerusalem (verse 32) *near their relatives*. Saul's descendants (verses 33-40) made no claim to the throne after the death of his sons, but apparently in later times they were active in the army (verse 40).

The Exile and After (9:1-34)

Verse 1 serves both as a close to the introductory section of genealogies and a preparation for the history from David to the restoration of Israel after their exile. The key phrase in the verse is *because of their unfaithfulness*. The Chronicler's history of Judah will emphasize that disaster is the consequence of any unfaithfulness to God.

Not only people of the tribes of *Judah* and *Benjamin*, near whose border *Jerusalem* was situated, but also people of the tribes of *Manasseh* and *Ephraim*, sons of Joseph, and the nucleus of the northern kingdom of Israel, came back to live in Jerusalem (9:3-9). Thus, the Holy City is again for all Israel, not just for Judah. Three branches of the tribe of *Judah* are listed, those of *Perez*, *Shelah* (the *Shilonites*) and *Zerah* (the *Zerahites*) (verses 4-6). Four branches of the Benjaminites are represented (verses 7-8).

The list of *the priests* is similar to Nehemiah's list of the priest families who returned to Jerusalem after the period of exile. After the three names that head the list, three priestly families are listed. The first branch is that of the high priests.

The Levites (9:14-16) were families whose men served as assistants to the priests. (See Nehemiah 11:15-18.) There seem to have been fewer Levites than priests. *The villages of the Netophathites* were a cluster near Bethlehem. Some of the first returnees to Jerusalem were natives of the region (Nehemiah 7:26).

The gatekeepers (9:17-27) are guards, porters, and maintainers at the Temple. The positions are inherited. More details of their function are given in 23:28-32. The prestige of their positions and work is enhanced with the knowledge that their forefathers had worked under

Phinehas. Phinehas was the grandson of Aaron, the brother of Moses. He was the high priest from whom all high priests of Israel were said to be descended.

The Chronicler describes the many services performed (9:28-32) by Temple servants, all of whom he considers to be Levite gatekeepers. *The musicians (singers)* (9:33) list of names seems to have been lost.

With verse 34 the introduction to the Chronicler's history ends.

§ § § § § § §

The Message of 1 Chronicles 6:1–9:34

Generations come and go. God's rule remains. Among the people of God are many who are forgotten or are known only through their relationships to the heads of families. Others are known only by their connection with some kind of service or by their residence in some particular place. Very few have been part of legends in popular tradition. Nevertheless, they are all part of the process of history that God ordains. The fact that they are God's chosen people, however, does not save them from disaster, destruction, or the complete loss of the land to which God led them, if they are unfaithful to God.

Still and all, God's choice of this people, the land God gave them for possession, God's purpose, God's rule and commandments, all remain for the people to return to.

The message still applies. Our value is in our participation, during our short time on earth, in the process of history toward the fulfillment of God's purpose. God never fails. We fail by failing God. We can return to God and resume our place in God's care and guidance.

§ § § § § § §

1 Chronicles 9:35–12:40

Introduction to These Chapters

This section starts with a brief narrative of the death of Saul, whose unfaithfulness made God put him and his line out of the way. David is pictured as the architect, under God's design, of that kingdom. He ascends the throne, captures Jerusalem, is surrounded by loyal *warriors,* and, endorsed by ever-increasing popular support, is crowned king of Israel.

David is a very talented, able leader of men, a good organizer and administrator, a folk hero; but mostly, for the Chronicler, a culmination in God's design for his people. Here is an outline of this section.

I. King Saul (9:35–10:14)
II. David's Kingship (11:1–12:40)
   A. The Choice of All Israel (11:1-3)
   B. David's Capture of Jerusalem (11:4-9)
   C. David's Warriors (11:10-47)
      1. The chiefs of David's mighty men (11:10-14)
      2. The daring loyalty of three (11:15-19)
      3. Exploits of Abishai and Benaiah (11:20-25)
      4. The list of war heroes (11:26-47)
   D. David's Supporters (12:1-22)
      1. Early supporters at Ziklag (12:1-7)
      2. Supporters at the stronghold (12:8-18)
      3. Manassite deserters to David (12:19-22)
   E. David's Coronation at Hebron (12:23-40)

King Saul (9:35–10:14)

The persons in his family tree were each a step toward Saul, Israel's first king. Therefore, the Chronicler begins his history of the kingdom of Israel with Saul's family tree, which he has already given in the Benjaminite genealogy (verses 29-38; see 1 Samuel 9:1).

Chronicles does not repeat what is found in 1 Samuel 9:17 and 10:1: that Saul was chosen and anointed by the Lord. If God had intended Saul to bring his people to their fulfillment in a righteous kingdom, then, from the Chronicler's point of view, Saul failed God. He tells nothing about the reign and life of Saul. He begins the history of an ideal reign, David's, with a brief reference to the end of a miserable reign, Saul's. Before the entry on stage of a faithful and worthy king, he tells about the end of a faithless, and therefore worthless, king. Out of the darkness represented by Saul emerges the brightness of David. Saul's death and David's glory also emphasize Chronicles' theme that faithlessness to God brings disaster, defeat, and exile, but faithfulness brings well-being, peace, and possession of the land.

In 1 Samuel 31:1-13, Saul's death is described as that of a hero, honored as a hero by his followers. Only a hint of this appears in the Chronicles account (verse 12). What is emphasized in Chronicles is Saul's total defeat and dishonor: the flight of his army; the loss of his towns, which were occupied by the enemy; his sons killed; his suicide; his head cut off by the enemy and hung in the temple of their god. This is the suffering and punishment brought about because he was unfaithful to the Lord (verse 13; see 1 Samuel 13:14). To make matters worse, he consulted a medium for guidance (as told in 1 Samuel 28:3-19). To seek guidance from the Lord is, for Chronicles, an essential for any leader of Israel. Therefore, God completely rejects Saul and his family from ever reigning in Israel. *All his house died together* (verse 6).

Actually Saul's son Ish-bosheth succeeded Saul as king over several of the tribes of Israel and he tried for two years to reign. The story is told in 2 Samuel 2–4. The Chronicler would know this and that there were descendants of Saul, already recorded in 9:39-44. What the Chronicler is saying is that from the point of view of God's purpose, Saul's family has been proven unworthy, incapable of being bearers of God's will for Israel.

The story gives a historical parallel to the more recent experience of Judah, referred to in 9:1: It was because of their unfaithfulness that Judah was taken into exile *(captivity)* in Babylon. They lost their king and their independence.

Therefore the LORD *put him to death, and turned the kingdom over to David* (verse 14). The kingdom is obviously God's. Kings are simply entrusted with its control, subject to their faithfulness.

The Choice of All Israel (11:1-3)

This account, corresponding to 2 Samuel 5:1-10, puts the emphasis on all Israel's choice of David. Defeated by the Philistines, facing collapse of the kingdom, they turn to their hero in battle. There is no mention of any dissidents. Ish-bosheth's reign collapses with his assassination. No mention is made that David reigns over Judah alone for seven and a half years in Hebron (2 Samuel 5:5). The Chronicler maintains the emphasis here, and consistently, that all twelve tribes of Israel are God's people, united in God's will. They choose David. Nevertheless, it is because David is God's choice that David *(will be the shepherd) of my people Israel.*

In fact, David's rule has been in God's planning: *according to the word of the* LORD *by Samuel* (NRSV; NIV = *as the* LORD *had promised through Samuel*). The Chronicler, whose Hebrew heritage includes the prophets, affirms that God's intentions for human history is made through the prophetic word. Moreover, David *made a covenant* (compact) *with them.* In a time when most rulers are despots who take control and maintain it by force, David makes a contract with the people. He must do so because the people of Israel are God's concern. The people pledge loyalty to David as God's choice for their ruler. The emphasis of Hebrew religion, which Chronicles maintains, is on a covenant offered by God, not demanded by the people.

David's Capture of Jerusalem (11:4-9)

Both the anointing of David as king by *all Israel* and the taking of *Jerusalem* are essential at the very beginning of the Chronicler's history, for his history is about God's kingdom under David and Solomon at Jerusalem. Other incidents along the way, recorded in the first four chapters of 2 Samuel, are therefore without importance to the Chronicler, and not mentioned.

Jerusalem is an ancient city, perhaps originally called Salem, city of peace (see Genesis 14:18). At the time David takes it, it is a city of the *Jebusites*; thus the Chronicler calls the city Jebus. It is ideally located for protection because it is a group of hills surrounded by valleys. Also, it is away from the natural highways north and south by which not only trade but also armies move. The walled citadel is on a high hill overlooking a brook in a valley. This is the Mount Zion that David captures and that comes to be called *the city of David.*

For many years, David's commander-in-chief is Joab. How he becomes leader of the army is explained here. Joab's act shows courage, initiative, and undoubtedly leadership. *Went up* was the phrase used for going into battle. Verse 8 pictures David and Joab rebuilding walls that they have breached, and repairing and protecting the area of residence around the citadel. Archaeologists have defined *the Millo* (NRSV) as the *supporting terraces* (NIV) that were built to support the houses on the steep eastern slope of the hill.

David became more and more powerful only because *the LORD of hosts* (NRSV; NIV = LORD Almighty) *was with him.* And the Lord is with him because David is faithful to God. LORD *of host*s is the title that expresses the absolute might and majesty of God as ruler over history

David's Warriors (11:10-47)

This passage and the following passage (Chapter 12) are written to show David's popular support. David has the support of his army, of all the people, *as the* LORD *had promised* (NIV; NRSV = *according to the word of the* LORD). Army leadership often chooses kings. Saul's general, on Saul's death, set up Ish-bosheth as king of Israel (2 Samuel 2:8-9). That choice, however, was not the Lord's choice. David's army, according to Chronicles (12:38), represents the will of the people. They represent the will of God (12:23). These chapters present a dramatic picture, like the opening of a great celebration, with group after group coming onto the scene, joining forces with David. The effect builds—to impress the reader-viewer of the drama—of the united support of David by all the people of Israel. The passage is drawn from 2 Samuel 23:8-39. It is a picture of a hero who can attract to himself daring and loyal comrades.

The Chiefs of David's Mighty Men (11:10-14)

The stories of David's *mighty men (warriors)* are from the period before he was king, when he was a popular hero in conflict with King Saul. There were *three* (some versions say thirty) mighty men who became legendary figures who headed the list of David's warriors. Two are named here: first, *Jashobeam*, second, *Eleazar*. The exploits that achieved their positions are told (verses 11, 14). Part of the original story (see 2 Samuel 23:8-12) was lost from Chronicles, so that the exploits of Eleazar and the name of the third hero, Shammah, were lost. Shammah's exploits appear to be Eleazar's in the present Chronicles version. For all their bravery, Chronicles points out that it was the Lord who gave them *a great victory.*

The Daring Loyalty of Three (11:15-19)
Verses 15-19 tell another daring exploit of three hero comrades of David. Their bravery is pictured, but more than that, their loyalty to David. His followers are in hiding from Saul in the cave of *Adullam*. Israel's enemy, the *Philistines*, have penetrated deep into Judah, as far as *Bethlehem*. *Rephaim*, the *valley of giants*, is near the city of Jerusalem.

Exploits of Abishai and Benaiah (11:20-25)
The extraordinary exploits of two more heroes have the color of stories told and retold and magnified in the process. Abishai is the *brother of Joab* whose exploit has already been told (verse 6). Benaiah struck down two of Moab's best men (NIV; NRSV = two sons of Ariel of Moab). Moab is east of the Dead Sea.

The List of War Heroes (11:26-47)
Two lists are used here. One (verses 26-41) probably predates the writing of Samuel (2 Samuel 23:24-39) and was several centuries old. The other list (verses 41-47) was unknown to Samuel. Most of the names are linked with some geographic place. Several are non-Israelite, notably *Uriah the Hittite*. The story of David's later affair with Uriah's wife Bathsheba, of Uriah's unwitting loyalty to David, and of David's arrangement for Uriah's death (2 Samuel 11:2-17) are not told in Chronicles, where any stories that might besmirch the great king's name are omitted.

Early Supporters at Ziklag (12:1-7)
Ziklag is a town in southern Judah, near Philistia. At this time it is owned by a Philistine king who, when David is outlawed by King Saul, gives it to David for a safe base of operation (1 Samuel 27:6). Many warriors and leaders from several places in Saul's own tribe of Benjamin, disenchanted with Saul, come over to David

while he is there. Their skills are described as exceptional with either their right or left hands. One of them, *Ishmaiah*, even becomes one of David's closest comrades-in-arms, part of the *thirty*.

Supporters at the Stronghold (12:8-18)

The stronghold in the desert (wilderness) (verses 8, 16): Before Ziklag, David moves about to different strongholds as hideout bases. Samuel mentions three locations: the cave of Adullam southwest of Jerusalem, En-gedi and Ziph in southern Judah. To these hideouts flock, according to Samuel, people in distress, in debt, and the discontented. A small army gathers around David (1 Samuel 22:1-5; 23:14; 23:29). The Chronicler mentions able warriors coming to him, warriors from Gad, east of the Jordan, and from the tribal territories of Judah and Benjamin. The description of the prowess of the Gadites, likened to that of *lions* and *gazelles*, is typical in heroic epic literature. The weakest of them is said to be a match for a *hundred*, the best, a match for *a thousand*. Their courage is shown in crossing *the Jordan* from their tribal territory in the time of the frightening springtime floods (verse 15).

How can David be sure that some who come to him might not be agents of Saul, pretending friendship in order to seize him? He will welcome their alliance with him: *I am ready to have you unite with me* (NIV; NRSV = *my heart will be knit to you*), but he warns them of God's judgment if they intend to betray him. Their reply in verse 18 is a beautiful expression of loyalty and peace. Not only will the people of Judah and Benjamin always be loyal to the house of David, but God is his helper. He is God's choice. This is said by inspiration. As Chronicles usually phrases it: *the Spirit came upon* him.

Manassite Deserters to David (12:19-22)

To understand these verses, read 1 Samuel 29. It is when David came with the Philistines to fight against Saul: the Philistine leaders suspect that David and his soldiers, allies of one of their chiefs, Achish by name, might turn against them in order to win favor with Saul. They know of his fame for able warfare. So they *sent him away*. It is on the way back from the Philistine army that *the men of Manasseh* (NIV; NRSV = *Messenites*), deserters from Saul's army, join David. Since the Philistines have gathered for a battle north of Manasseh at Jezreel in northern Israel (1 Samuel 29:11), David will be returning south through Manasseh toward his base in Ziklag when the Manassites join him. They are army leaders, *chiefs (leaders)* of the land. The dissolution of Saul's army is apparent. On his return to Ziklag, according to 1 Samuel 30, David finds that his city has been raided and burned by a band of nomadic Amalekites who live to the south of Judah. David goes after them and recovers the property and the people they have captured. The Manassites, says Chronicles, *helped* him (verse 21). Others continue to come down from Manasseh *to help him*, until there was *a great army, like the army of God*, because David has God's help.

David's Coronation at Hebron (12:23-40)

The Chronicler returns the story to Hebron, south of Jerusalem, where *all Israel* gathers, determined to make David king (verse 38). This passage pictures great troops coming from every tribe to join those who are already in David's army. The latter provided for the coming of the crowds to celebrate (verse 39), and those who come bring caravans of food and animals (verse 40). Interesting comments are made about the different bands who come. They are listed by tribe, first those in the south, then those in the north, and last those to the northeast on the other side of the Jordan. The picture is that of all Israel, united in order to make David king.

One tribal distinction is made. The priests of the Levite tribe are separately mentioned (verse 27). Even King Saul's own kin join support for David (verse 29). Three days they were *eating and drinking* together—an experience of communion, a covenant meal—of one great family (verse 39), who reach out and include their *neighbors* (verse 40). These are expressions of unity, so important in Chronicles.

§ § § § § § §

The Message of 1 Chronicles 9:35–12:40

The passage begins with the family tree of Saul. Generations come and go. God's righteous purpose endures, and by it human life stands or falls. By failing God, unfaithful to him, Saul fell.

The passage continues with the people's choice of David. This choice began when David was an outlaw chief because the king, Saul, wished to kill him on account of his great popularity with the people. It shows how group after group of warriors joined David until the time came when all of Israel was for him. It points out that the army's choice of their leader, David, was also all the people's choice, and it was God's choice. It emphasizes that the king is chosen by God, and that he is entrusted with God's rule of the people.

The continuing message of this section of Chronicles is that God rules history in righteousness, and he chooses those who will be faithful to his righteousness. God does not protect those who are unfaithful from the consequences of their own actions. He allows the course of human conflict to punish them. God does not support human choices that are contrary to his will. He does support human choices that carry out his choice. God honors those who are daring and courageous to do his will.

God's choice is for the solidarity of his people. As they join together to do God's will and to support his choice, God will bless them so that they may live together in unity and greatness.

§ § § § § § §

PART FOUR 1 Chronicles 13–20

Introduction to These Chapters

The *ark of the covenant,* representing the presence of God, was the focus of all Israel in its journey to, and its establishment in, the land of Canaan. David recognizes this and wishes to bring the ark from the sanctuary where it rests in Kiriath-jearim to his capital, Jerusalem. The journey of the ark to Jerusalem is made in two stages (chapters 13 and 15). Between these two stages, David has three proofs that he has God's blessing: (1) King Hiram of Phoenicia sends him materials to build his palace, (2) he is blessed with many children, and (3) he is able, by his military victories, to establish himself as a power in the region (chapter 14).

Here is an outline of chapters 13–20.
  I. Bringing the Ark from Kiriath-jearim (13:1-14)
 II. David's House and Home (14:1-7)
III. Victories Over the Philistines (14:8-15)
 IV. The Ark of God in Zion (15:1–16:43)
     A. Bringing the ark to Zion (15:1-29)
     B. Worship at the ark of the Lord (16:1-43)
  V. David's Desire to Build a Temple (17:1-15)
 VI. David's Prayer (17:16-27)
VII. The House of David (18:1–20:8)
     A. David's conquests (18:1-13)
     B. David's government (18:14-17)
     C. Campaign against the Ammonites (19:1–20:3)
     D. David's heroes against the Philistines (20:4-8)

Bringing the Ark from Kiriath-jearim (13:1-14)

The ark of our God is a simple chest of acacia wood (Deuteronomy 10:3). It represents the presence of God in Israel, and it reflects God's power (1 Samuel 4:3–7:2).

These verses contain four prominent themes of the Chronicler. First is the absolute importance of reverence and worship of God at the heart of Israel's life. Second is the solidarity of all Israel about that center. The phrases in these verses stress that solidarity: *all the assembly of Israel . . . our brothers (kindred) . . . all the land (territories) of Israel . . . come together to us (come and join us) . . . the whole assembly agreed . . . because it seemed right to all the people (for the thing pleased all the people). So David assembled all Israel* (verses 2-5). The assembling of Israel is frequent in Chronicles (11:1-3; 23:2; 28:1; 2 Chronicles 1:2-3; 5:2). A third theme is that every reaction of the king must be in accord with the will of the people and of God. A fourth theme is the important place of the *priests and Levites* in any religious activity.

From Shihor to *Hamath* is the extent of David's empire, from Egypt to far north of Lebanon. *Kiriath-jearim* was several miles west of Jerusalem.

Verses 6-14 parallel 2 Samuel 6:2-11. The participation of all of Israel (verses 6, 8) is repeated. The *cherubim* were small symbolic figures, probably winged like the *wings of the wind* (Psalm 18:10) but of form unknown today, which stood at each end of the cover of the ark where God's awesome presence was enthroned above them.

Verse 8 pictures the religious ecstasy of the people. Verse 9 shows the awesome power of the ark. What the driver, *Uzzah*, does seems natural enough, but it is improper. His act does not recognize the potency of the ark, just as one might automatically reach out to make an adjustment of an electric line and be electrocuted. The tragedy puts a chill on the rejoicing.

David was angry and *afraid* at the same time (verses 11-12). His anticipation is shattered for the time being.

God has broken out against *Uzzah* (the meaning of *Perez-uzzah*, verse 11). God's immense power is usually contained, because it is too much for a creature to bear. But occasionally it breaks out (see also in 14:11). The celebration comes to a stop. The ark is lodged in a nearby house of a Levite (15:18), *Obed-edom the Gittite* (that is, from the city of Gath). The power emanating from the ark blesses and benefits his home (verse 14).

David's House and Home (14:1-7)

God's breaking forth on Uzzah shocks David into uncertainty about the confident action he has taken. Can he presume to bring the power of God's presence to his capital at Jerusalem? The Chronicler inserts at this point the account in 2 Samuel 5:11-25 to show the reassurance given to David. He is under God's blessing because of his desire to have the ark of God, putting God's presence foremost in his kingship.

One blessing, the munificent gift of the king of Tyre in Phoenicia, awakens David to his own acceptance as a great king. The cedar trees of Lebanon were, until recent time, famous building material. Note that David's kingdom is highly exalted *for the sake of his people Israel* (verse 2). The king is no despot, but entrusted by God to rule God's people.

A second blessing is children. The greater the king, it was assumed, the more wives and concubines he could have (verse 3); a large family was a sign of divinely blessed prosperity.

Victories over the Philistines (14:8-15)

The third evidence of God's blessing is David's victories in war. *The Philistines* fight against the king of *all Israel*. In pre-monarchic days the Philistine method was to raid various tribes. This time, their daring raids in a valley near Jerusalem (*Rephaim*, verse 9) are met head-on by David. It happens, however, only after David seeks direction from God (verse 10), an essential, according to Chronicles, for any successful action.

Warring peoples carried their gods into battle to assure victory. The gods that David captures from the Philistines, evidence that his God is greater, are burned according to Hebrew law (see Deuteronomy 7:5).

Another raid by the Philistines is again met successfully. Again, however, David does not act without seeking God's direction and following the strategy that God gives him (verses 14-16). As usual, it is God who gives the victory. The Philistines are driven back from *Gibeon*, north of Jerusalem, to *Gezer*, in Philistine territory. The consequence of David's faithfulness to God is his fame among the nations (verse 17).

Bringing the Ark to Zion (15:1-29)

David is now ready to bring *the ark of God* to Jerusalem, and he prepares a place for its coming. This action parallels 2 Samuel 6:12-20. This time the bringing of the ark will be in the proper hands. No one but the Levites may carry it, as required (verse 13) by the Mosaic commandment (verse 15). Even they would not be safe doing so unless they cleansed themselves in a ceremony of sanctification (verses 12, 14). The Levite families, by descent, are listed in verses 5-10. Verses 5-7 are similar to the list in chapter 6. The names of *Zadok* and *Abiathar* have been added. (See 2 Samuel 15:24-29 for their story.)

The ark was made with loops so that it could be carried *with the poles* (see Exodus 25:13-15). *The word of the LORD* always conveys the idea of God's commandments, will, or Spirit.

Again we have the procession with the sound of musical instruments and singing (verses 16, 27-28). At this time, according to the Chronicler, the singing guilds of *Heman, Asaph,* and *Ethan* are appointed. Ethan is sometimes called *Jeduthun* as in 16:41-42. These guilds will, from now on, accompany all worship celebrations with psalms and music. *Obed-edom*—the name first appears as a citizen of the Philistine city of Gath—is listed as a Levite gatekeeper (verses 18-24) and a musician on the lyre (verse 21). The *bronze cymbals* beat the time. *Harps according to Alamoth* are the soprano sounds. *Lyres according to Sheminith* are the bass, an octave or more below the harps. Verse 24 inserts *the priests were to blow the trumpets* to be in accord with Numbers 10:8.

The procession (15:25–16:3) parallels 2 Samuel 6:12-19. David and the people are dressed in festive garments.

Worship at the Ark of the Lord (16:1-43)

In this passage, the Chronicler describes the ideal of Israelite worship, and attributes its organization to David. It is worship led by Levites (a later editor adds *priests* in verses 6, 39). It is sung worship with songs of invocation (the psalms of lament), of thanksgiving, and of praise. The author selects parts of three beautiful psalms from the book of Psalms. Verses 8-22 equal Psalm 105:1-15; verses 23-33 equal Psalm 96:1-13; verse 34 equals Psalm 106:1; and verses 35-36 equal Psalm 106:47-48. These psalms echo the Chronicler's themes of seeking the Lord (verse 11), God's chosen people (verses 13, 22), and God's covenant with the people (verses 15-17). They express joyous gratitude that God has chosen, delivered, and loved Israel, and has covenanted with Israel. *All the earth* is to worship God (verse 23). This emphasis, characteristic of prophets much later than David's time, the Chronicler finds appropriate for a united Israel in his own time.

By tradition, the tent of meeting used by Israel in its desert crossing remains in *Gibeon* (verses 39-42).

David's Desire to Build a Temple (17:1-15)

The Chronicler's chief concern is the building of the Temple. This chapter begins with David's desire to build a temple, the prophet Nathan's message from God, and David's response (see 2 Samuel 7).

Nathan the prophet is King David's spiritual advisor. What God says to David through Nathan stresses the primary and initiating action of God. God raised up David to *be ruler over my people Israel* (verse 7). God gave him victory over his enemies (verses 8, 10). God gives a home to Israel (verse 9) and to David (verses 9-10). God appointed their judges (verse 10), and God will raise a son to David who will build the Temple (verses 11, 12). All is very much in God's hands and control. Verse 10 is important. David cannot build God's house, but God will subdue all his enemies. Then, and after David's death, the time will be right for building God's house. God is eternal, and will establish David's line forever. He can be sure of God's unchanging love. *Him who was before you* (NRSV; NIV = *your predecessor*) is King Saul.

Verse 14 seems to be a promise of an unending dynasty. When Chronicles was written, that dynasty had ended. But the reign of David and of Solomon remained forever as the ideal kingdom of God.

David's Prayer (17:16-27)

This prayer comes almost verbatim from 2 Samuel 7. Samuel's David frequently prays. This habit is found often among faithful persons through all of Chronicles (see 2 Chronicles 6). The prayer reflects on the greatness of God, whose name will be established and remain great for ever. God's greatness is reflected in the choice of Israel *to be his people* redeemed *from Egypt* (the Exodus). The permanence of God's covenant with the people and with the house of David is frequently repeated (verses 13-14, 22-24, 27). What the Lord has blessed is *blessed for ever* (verse 27).

David's Conquests (18:1-13)

In chapters 18–20, the Chronicler has compressed the story told in 2 Samuel 8–21. Warfare is David's task.

Israel cannot build a temple to God while tormented by enemies. David must subdue them, and God *gave victory to David everywhere he went* (verse 6). His engagement in bloodshed, however, makes him unfit to build God's house. He will prepare Israel through conquest and prosperity for the building of the temple. He dedicates the spoils of war to the temple.

David's empire extends from Zobah, as far as Hamath and the Aramean kingdom of Damascus in the north, east of Lebanon, south to the Amalekites. The Amalekites live in the desert south of Judah and south of Edom and the Dead Sea. David rules from Gath in Philistia on the west to Moab and the Ammonites east of the Dead Sea.

David's Government (18:14-17)

This record is from 2 Samuel 8:15-18 with emphasis on responsible kingship, *justice and equity* (NRSV; NIV = *doing what was just and right*) to all God's people. The records indicate that David is an efficient manager. The officers of his government includes (1) *Joab:* commander of the army; (2) *Jehoshaphat:* the king's chief secretary who probably counsels the king, administers his orders, and records his decrees and judgments; (3) *Zadok* and *Ahimelech:* high priests; (4) *Shavsha:* secretary in charge of legal documents. The *Cherethites (Kerethites)* and *Pelethites* are David's bodyguard, the core of his royal army. The king's sons gain experience as administrators.

Campaign Against the Ammonites (19:1–20:3)

This story is found in 2 Samuel 10. The *Ammonites* live east of northern Israel, between Gilead and the desert. They are a Semitic people who occasionally make incursions into Gilead. When David, outlawed, was fighting Saul, *Nahash,* their king, was glad to help him. When Nahash dies, therefore, David is ready to offer friendship to his son and successor, *Hanun.* The shaving of heads and the cutting off of garments are considered shaming insults. Knowing there will be reprisals, Hanun quickly buys armaments and hires an army from neighboring kingdoms and draws Syria into an alliance. *Mesopotamia* (Naharaim), *Aram-maacah,* and *Zobah* are north of Ammon in what is largely Syria today. The Syrian allies (verses 16-19) are from farther east. *Medeba* is a Moabite city south of Ammon, but may be in Ammonite hands at this time. The figures, in epic style, are exaggerated.

Verse 1 of chapter 20 is an interesting comment on ancient politics. Raids, ravaging enemy neighbors' countrysides, were perennial. This battle is more than a raid, however. It is a revenge war. So *Rabbah,* the Ammonite capital, is besieged and, when it is taken, David feels justified in sacking the city and enslaving its people as he did to all the Ammonite towns. Rabbah continues today as Amman, the capital of Jordan.

In verse 3, David and his army returned to Jerusalem. This note assumes the fuller story in 2 Samuel 12:26-31. Chronicles omits the story of David's affair with Bathsheba that, according to 2 Samuel, took place when Joab and the army were in Ammon.

David's Heroes Against the Philistines (20:4-8)

The stories of David's wars end with the accounts of the frequent battles with the Philistines. They are typical folk-legends and may come from a collection of tales of David and his men, beginning with his outlaw days (see 1 Chronicles 11).

The *Rephaites* (NIV; NRSV = *descendants of the giants*) may have been descendants from a tall race of aborigines who occupied the area before it was overrun by Canaanites, the predecessors of the invading Philistines.

Gezer and *Gath* (*Gittite* means someone from Gath) are two cities in eastern Philistia. The spear *like a weavers beam (rod)* (verse 5), and the giant's taunts (verse 7) are applied to Goliath in 1 Samuel 17:8-9.

§ § § § § § §

The Message of 1 Chronicles 13–20

This portion of 1 Chronicles is about a three-way relationship between God, David, and the people. What David does is related to the worship and will of God, and to God's people. David's major concern is to get the ark of God, the symbol of God's presence, into Jerusalem. He fails at first, but tries again and succeeds. He leads the people in celebrating God in songs of thanksgiving and praise. His desire to build a temple to God in his capital is thwarted because his nation is surrounded by enemies, and the land has no rest. By the power of God he overwhelms his enemies and extends the rule of Israel over its neighbors.

The message of this portion is:

§ Bring to the center of life that which makes us aware of God's presence and power.

§ Give God the credit for all that is good in life.

§ If you have failed to center your attention on God, seek a deeper awareness of God.

§ Celebrate the joy of God's presence with God's people in song, prayer, thanksgiving, and praise.

§ Put foremost in life the desire to worship God.

§ Seek God's guidance in every undertaking.

§ Put your life in God's hands. If you have a goal for God's glory that you are unable to achieve, prepare the way for someone else to achieve it.

§ Let your actions be directed by God, dependent on God, and dedicated to God.

§ Whatever of value comes to you, donate it to God.

§ Manage your affairs responsibly for God's glory.

§ Remember those who have been kind and helpful to you, and pass on the kindness.

§ § § § § § §

1 Chronicles 21:1–23:1

Introduction to These Chapters

David wishes to build the Temple as the crowning act of his reign (chapter 17), but his attention has been turned to the conquest of enemies (chapters 18–21). Chapter 21 is related to his military campaigns. He wishes to make a census of all Israel, including conquered lands, to discover the number of men capable of military service.

A national epidemic follows the census. This disaster, and David's reaction to it, becomes the occasion by which David discovers where the temple will be built. He gathers and prepares material and workmen for the building and charges and advises Solomon and Israel's leadership on the building of the temple (chapter 22).

Here is an outline of these chapters.
  I. The Military Census (21:1–22:1)
     A. David's census (21:1-6)
     B. Israel's punishment (21:7-14)
     C. David's penitent plea (21:15-17)
     D. The threshing floor of Ornan (21:18–22:1)
 II. Preparing for the Temple of the Lord (22:2–23:1)
     A. Materials and workers (22:2-5)
     B. David's charge to Solomon (22:6-16)
     C. Charge to the leaders of Israel (22:17–23:1)

The Military Census (21:1–22:1)

The Chronicler adapts the story in 2 Samuel 24 to make his message clear to his contemporaries. The census and the resulting epidemic prepare the way for the story in 21:28–22:1, the discovery of a holy place for God's temple. There are two reports (Numbers 1 and 26) of military censuses in Israel (Numbers 1:3). There is no prohibition in the books of the law against taking a census. There was an ancient fear that to number a people would be to risk a plague that would decimate them. Josephus, a Jewish historian of the first century A.D., suggests that David's mistake in taking the census is that he does not charge this tax. According to the Chronicler, however, David's error is that, by taking the military census, he is depending on manpower for Israel's defense, rather than on the Lord.

David's Census (21:1-6)

Satan (verse 1), instead of *the* LORD (2 Samuel 24:1), *incited David to number* (NRSV; NIV = *take a census of*) *Israel. Satan* is from a Hebrew root that means *to accuse* or *to obstruct*. Satan is an adversarial spirit, even a human frailty, that can incite even good people to do that which is contrary to God's will. Nevertheless, God can use that incitement, as this chapter will show, to bring about divine purpose. The census, a military census (verse 5), is for the purpose of conscription *from Beersheba to Dan* (verse 2), from the southernmost part to the northern end of Israel.

Joab, for the Chronicler, becomes David's antagonist in taking the census (verses 3, 6), yet he loyally obeys his king (verse 4). *He did not include Levi* (verse 6). The law (Numbers 1:49) excluded the Levites from military census.

Israel's Punishment (21:7-14)

God struck Israel (verse 7) with a *pestilence (plague)* (verse 14). The pestilence, a serious epidemic that kills such large numbers, is taken as evidence of God's displeasure. David so takes it and is aghast at what he, apparently, caused by his census. It is David's sin, but David and the people are inseparably related. So he prays for his nation.

Gad, like Nathan, is a religious counselor. Every king's court had *seer* who were thought to have a special contact with a nation's deity. Unlike them, David's counselors are related to a God the Hebrews conceived of as all-powerful in righteousness. Morality is involved. David chooses (verse 13) what seems to be, at least in duration, the lesser of the three punishments the Lord offers. It is better to be in the hands of an angry God of mercy than in those of merciless human foes.

David's Penitent Plea (21:15-17)

In verse 15, the Lord relented and stopped the angel. There are other biblical notes of God's relenting after seeing the results of a decision (Genesis 6:6; Exodus 32:14; 1 Samuel 15:35; Jonah 3:10). As in Psalm 106:45, God relents because *of his steadfast (great) love* for the people.

The concept of an angel that destroys or a destroying deity was, and still is, common to most religious cultures as an explanation of deadly disease. *Sackcloth*, a rough weaving of goat's or camel's hair, was worn as a loincloth in place of the usual clothing, as a sign of mourning, or by all the people as an expression of penitence and humiliation after a public disaster, or to plead for its removal (see Jonah 3:5-6). David, the former shepherd, refers to his people as *sheep*. The cry to spare them and to punish himself alone (verse 17) for a wrong that he alone had done shows a high moral sensitivity beyond the common ethics of the time. (See Abraham's compassionate concern that innocent people should not suffer for the evil of others, in Genesis 18:22-32.)

The Threshing Floor of Ornan (21:18–22:1)

The point of the story for the Chronicler is that the angel was standing at the threshing floor of Ornan

(Araunah), the Jebusite (verse 15). It is here that David is commanded to build an altar to the Lord. It is here that David makes *burnt offerings and fellowship offerings* (NIV; NRSV = *offerings of well-being*), so that Ornan's threshing floor becomes the center of national worship performed, in Israel's behalf, by the king. Ornan (Araunah in the 2 Samuel spelling) is a Jebusite, a member of the people who lived in Jerusalem before David captured it for his capital (11:4-9). The place is atop a hill just north of the original *city of David* and opposite the Mount of Olives.

At first Ornan seems to be unmoved by the sight of the angel. Is it devotion or fear that makes Ornan offer the king not only his threshing floor, but his oxen and threshing sledges and wheat and all he has? This offer throws in relief David's need to buy it all for *its full price*. Thus the sacrifice can be at his great cost and so be effective. The *six hundred shekels of gold by weight* is a round figure for a huge sum of money. The sacrifice is effective. It is not, however, the sacrifice itself—as would be the case in most oriental religions—but the Lord who stops the epidemic. God, for the Chronicler, is always in charge.

Tradition held that the tent of meeting, which Moses made (Exodus 25–27) to accompany the Israelites on their journey from Egypt, still stood at *Gibeon* in a *high place* (the usual location of worship altars) in a town in Benjamin, northwest of Jerusalem. Why does David not go there to make his sacrifice to save Israel? Because, the Chronicler explains, *he was afraid of the sword of the angel of the* LORD (verse 30). At the angel's direction, through the prophet Gad, he offers the sacrifice on Ornan's threshing floor. This act justifies replacing the old center of worship at Gibeon with the new. Now David understands how God has been leading him.

Materials and Workers (22:2-5)

David gathers building materials in Jerusalem. He impresses alien residents and conquered people into work crews (20:3). The reason he gives for going ahead with preparations instead of leaving them to Solomon: *my son is young and inexperienced* (verse 5). This reason corresponds to young Solomon's response to God, according to 1 Kings 3:7. David is having the building materials put into shape. The stone (verse 2) is probably limestone; the iron from mines in conquered Philistia; bronze, silver, and gold captured in his wars (18:8, 11; 20:2). The cedars are from great trees that covered the forest mountains of Lebanon to the north. The Chronicler speaks of the large quantities of materials and the magnificence of David's design.

David's Charge to Solomon (22:6-16)

David's urgent concern to build the temple and his explanation, both of the reasons he cannot do so and of his preparations for the building, are given in three charges—one to his son, Solomon (22:6-16), a second to *all the leaders of Israel* calling them to assist Solomon (22:17-19), and a third in a public assembly (28:1-8).

From chapter 17 on, *a house for the LORD* dominates Chronicles. Chapters 18–20 were about wars, but they were fought to prepare the nation for the rest that was the essential environment in which the temple could be built (see Deuteronomy 12:9-11 and 1 Chronicles 17:9). Now that David has made all his preparations, he commits the task of building the temple to his son, Solomon.

First, David explains the hope he had to build the temple and the reason he could not. This is the first full explanation: He had shed so much blood. Blood is the essence of life and the shedding of it is the negation of life. That is why the Hebrew people were forbidden to eat · blood and from coming before the tent of meeting without being purified of blood pollution (see Leviticus 17:8-16).

Bloodshed has polluted David, and worse, it was shed before the Lord (verse 8). Not only did he shed blood, but he had fought many wars and so was a man of violence, even though he had done these things under the direction and with the aid of the Lord. The ideal state will be one of peace, allowing security and prosperity and great gatherings for worship and religious celebration.

David explains, in words Nathan spoke from the Lord (17:11-14), his choice of Solomon to *build a house for my name*. The Chronicler has been careful, in 17:3-8, to avoid any idea that God would be confined in this house. (Indeed, it is God who gives a place and a house to the people, 17:9-10.) It is also not David, but God, who gives Solomon *peace* (that is, rest from turmoil) and establishes his *throne* (verses 9, 10). His name is to be Solomon (verse 9), which means, in Hebrew, *peaceful*.

David's charge begins with a wish, a prayer that God will grant him *discretion and understanding* and that he *keep the law of the LORD your God* (verse 12). The Chronicler's confidence in cause and effect follows in the words, *Then you will prosper (have success) if you . . . observe . . . (that) which the LORD commanded . . . for Israel* (verse 13). Then follows the charge that in building the house of the LORD your God (verse 11) and in his reign over Israel (verse 12), he be strong and courageous . . . do not be afraid or discouraged: These are standard biblical phrases of encouragement (see Deuteronomy 31:7, 8, 23; Joshua 1:6-9). David's thorough preparations for a great temple are indicated by the exaggerated list of materials supplied, and the description of workers of various skills.

Charge to the Leaders of Israel (22:17–23:1)

Like the first charge to Solomon, this charge shows David's great desire to have the temple built, and his anxiety, typical of energetic people, that someone other that he (that is, Solomon) be able to carry it out. Although Chronicles always asserts the help of God as an essential to any successful enterprise, that does not preclude David's asking the leaders of God's people *to help Solomon his son*. In fact, they should help because God is with them and has given them *rest (peace)* from attack from neighboring nations (verse 18).

To *seek* the Lord is a recurrent emphasis in Chronicles. The *holy vessels* are the utensils used for sacrifices and incense in the old tabernacle (21:29). Verse 23:1 is an added conclusion.

§ § § § § § §

The Message of 1 Chronicles 21:1–23:1

David follows an impulse, without consulting God, to take a military census of Israel. God is displeased and punishes Israel. David is distressed that others are suffering when he alone is to blame. He prays for forgiveness. God forgives. Forgiveness restores the relationship, but does not free the wrongdoer from the results of his wrong. A man of decision and action, David is prevented by God's will from building the temple himself, but does all he can to prepare his successor-son, Solomon, and the leaders of his country to build the Temple.

The message says to all people in all periods:

§ Live daily in complete dependence on God.

§ Be ready to admit and repent of mistakes.

§ Regret not that you suffer for wrong you have done, but that the wrong separates you from God.

§ Prefer that you, not others, suffer for your wrongdoing.

§ Make the worship of God your first concern.

§ Willingly share your ideas, plans, hopes with others who can carry them out.

§ Urge others who are leaders in society to keep God's commandments and be faithful to God.

§ § § § § § §

1 Chronicles 23:2–26:32

Introduction to These Chapters

The last part of 1 Chronicles deals with the end of David's reign. It omits the personal and political events recorded in 1 Kings 1–2. It reports mostly what relates to the worship of God in the Temple. It makes pointedly clear that it was David who organized the Levites for the Temple service, although scholars believe that this organization was much later.

Mixed into these lists is the division of priests, as well as of Levites, into twenty-four *courses*. The Temple duties rotate through the year among these courses so that there is continual worship of God, each division coming in to relieve the previous week's division, following the rituals prescribed in the Books of the Law.

Here is an outline of these chapters.
  I. David's Organization of the Levites (23:1-6)
 II. The Families of Temple Levites (23:7-32)
III. The Descendants of Aaron (24:1-19)
 IV. The Rest of the Levites (24:20-31)
  V. The Levite Musicians (25:1-31)
 VI. The Gatekeepers (26:1-19)
VII. Treasury Keepers (26:20-28)
VIII. Officers and Judges (26:29-32)

David's Organization of the Levites (23:1-6)

He made Solomon his son king (verse 1). Thus, the Chronicler abbreviates the story told in 1 Kings 1:32-40.

As it stands, it appears that David, the old man, frees his hands of day-to-day government concerns so that he can devote himself to putting everything in order for his son's role in building the temple.

David assembled: From here on, whenever an important religious need or decision arises, the Chronicler will note that the king gathers together the people, or the leaders of the people, to initiate a program or to call for prayer and worship. *Thirty years old or more:* The prescribed age of service, according to Numbers 4:3, is *from thirty years old up to fifty years old,* but this may be a general figure because elsewhere the service-entering age is given as twenty (verses 24, 27; and 2 Chronicles 31:17). *Were counted* for religious service is not the same as the military census condemned in chapter 21.

Verses 4-6 summarize the four divisions (but from three family lines [verse 6]) of Levites. This list reflects the organization of Levites in the days of the Chronicler, who says that their organization goes back to the days of David: (1) Those in charge of the work in the Lord's Temple. This involves assistance to the priests in their ritual duties, and in custodial and maintenance responsibilities as outlined in verses 28-32. (2) *Officers* (or scribes) *and judges,* (3) *gatekeepers,* (4) singers and players of musical instruments, and leaders in psalms and prayers. The Chronicler will give this small group of Levites special attention for their importance in worship.

The Families of Temple Levites (23:7-32)

These are the names of those serving in the temple supposedly at David's time, together with the abbreviated list of their genealogies. *Sons of* means *descendants,* many generations being skipped, only the most prominent persons being named. *Heads of the families* indicates that the list is only (except where specifically mentioned) of the line of the firstborn sons of firstborn sons. Workers and singers at shrines and the temple, even some of foreign origin, came to be incorporated into Levite family genealogies.

Someone wishing to give separate prominence to *priests* from ordinary Levites has added the sentence about *Aaron . . . and his sons* (verses 13-14).

Verse 24 sums up the list. Verse 25 starts a new passage. Verses 28-32, (skipping verse 27, which is parenthetical) attempt, like verse 13, to insist on the distinction of priests from other Levites, and the relatively lower level and limited service of the Levites. Note the emphasis on daily thanking and praising the Lord.

The Descendants of Aaron (24:1-19)

A later writer than the original Chronicler builds from verse 13 in chapter 23 information about the order of priests. The only Levites who can serve as priests are descendants of Aaron. The sixteen divisions of the larger or more important family of Eleazar, and the eight of the family of Ithamar, make for the twenty-four divisions that divide up the annual periods of temple duty through the year. By the writer's time, they were organized *by lot* (verse 5).

Although *David* organized them according to the appointed duties in their service (verse 3), the summary (verse 19) says that their divisional duty of service was established for them by *Aaron*. Only in Chronicles are priests called *officers* (NRSV; NIV = *officials*) *of the sanctuary and officers of God* (verse 5). No known functional distinction between these is known, although each of the two rival houses of priests, the houses of Eleazar and of Ithamar, may have thus distinguished themselves. *Zadok* (verse 6) was prominent in the history of the reigns of David and Solomon.

The Rest of the Levites (24:20-31)

The writer who added the priest lists above (verses 1-19) here brings the Chronicler's list (23:6-23) up to date in his own time by adding current names to each branch of the family, except that he omits the list of the Gershom family entirely (which appears in 23:7-11). He implies (verse 31) that the Levites, like the priests, *cast lots* for the assignments of their own twenty-four divisions. In addition, no one, by virtue of being older, had any advantage of choice over the younger. This was done in the presence of *King David, Zadok, Ahimelech:* Ahimelech was the son of Abiathar, who served jointly with Zadok as David's priest. In this way, the record begun in chapter 23 is concluded, returning to the picture in 23:2.

The Levite Musicians (25:1-31)

Here are listed the leading musicians' families, those of Asaph, Heman, and Jeduthun. Other lists include the family of Korah, with whom some of the psalms are associated. Some singers, such as Heman (verse 5), were known as *seers,* whose spiritual vision, insights, and confident oracles made them counselors to the king.

In verses 1-7 the most famous musician families are listed, together with their instruments. Verses 8-31 divide them up into the twenty-four divisions for temple duty periods. Musicians are also listed in 15:16-24.

The Gatekeepers (26:1-19)

In the Chronicler's list of Levites, the gatekeepers follow the musicians. They are the security personnel (9:26-27). In the days before the temple, they were the carriers of the tabernacle and of the ark, the box that held the covenant. It is their duty, by turns, to keep *watch* at the gates of the temple at all times (verse 17). The *parbar* (verse 18) may have been a colonnade to the west of the temple proper.

Three families of gatekeepers are listed but only two with genealogies, the descendants of Korah (verse 1) and of Merari (verse 10). Obed-edom had many sons because *God blessed him* (verses 4-5; see 13:14). Verse 6 speaks of elders chosen in each extended family for their ability, not necessarily as a birthright (verse 10). The list differs from a list of gatekeepers in 9:17-27. They *cast lots* to determine the gates and the times each division would watch (verses 13-19). According to 23:3-6, they were appointed by David.

Treasury Keepers (26:20-28)

Not *Ahijah* (a mistranslation), but *fellow-Levites, had charge of the treasuries*. They are Levites of the families listed in 23:12-20. *Shebuel* (verse 24) is over all the treasuries. There are two treasuries: those *of the house of God*, and *of the dedicated gifts* (NRSV; NIV = *things*). This latter is a recipient of gifts made by kings and army leaders from the spoil won in battles (verses 26-28; see 18:7-8). They are used for the maintenance of the temple. *Abner* was King Saul's commander of the army. *Joab* was King David's commander (verse 28). Two different Levite families (verses 22 and 26) *were in charge of* the two treasuries.

Officers and Judges (26:29-32)

David can rely on loyal, able administrators among the *Hebronites* and the Levites in Levitical cities (cities set apart for Levites) throughout Israel. The judges and their officers have religious oversight (although not precisely defined) over *all the work of the LORD* (verse 30). Outside duties are those not related to the temple itself but to the law of the Lord, called the Torah, which is the religious, civil, and criminal code of Israel. Deuteronomy 17:8-9 gives a picture of the judge's duties.

For religious judicial oversight, as well as for civil affairs of the king, Israel is divided between all of Israel *west of the Jordan* (verse 30) and that part of Israel east of the Jordan (verse 32). *The fortieth year of David's reign* (verse 31) is his last year according to 1 Kings 2:11. *Jazer* is one of the cities reserved for Levites to live in.

§ § § § § § §

The Message of 1 Chronicles 23–26

According to this portion, King David, near the end of his life, and for the sake of his people, put his kingdom's house in order. His first concern was for the temple and the worship of God. For that reason he gave primary attention to the organization of the Levites, the people whose hereditary responsibility it was to guide the religious life of Israel. He organized and appointed them in twenty-four divisions of priests and non-priest Levites so that religious service was continuous. Thus the ideal kingdom had an ideal religious order with priests, musicians to lead in worship, gatekeepers to guard the temple, and judges and officers to interpret and apply the holy law.

The Chronicler's message was intended to show to the people of his time what the ideal theocratic state should be. Applicable to all time are his ideals that the people of God should:

§ live together in a well-ordered religious life.

§ in all things give pre-eminence to the worship of God.

§ let praise and thanksgiving be paramount in worship.

§ make music a large part of worship, singing to the Lord, playing instruments to praise God and to arouse spiritual fervor, devotion, and understanding.

§ share religious duties, all taking turns.

§ have persons among them who, as students of God's law, are able to administer and interpret it for the people in order to maintain right human relationships.

§ pass on the responsibilities of the religious life as a heritage from generation to generation.

§ § § § § § §

1 Chronicles 27–29

Introduction to These Chapters

Chapters 23–26 are germane to the Chronicler's theme: the organization of worship for the temple soon to be built. They contain the Chronicler's record of the persons who assist in worship—the Levites—and their tasks. Chapter 27 is a digression about general military and civil administration of David's reign. Nevertheless, it carries forward the record of orderliness in the ideal kingdom.

Chapters 28 and 29 return to the main theme, the preparation for the construction of the temple. The setting is given for Solomon's prosperous succession as King David dies.

These chapters may be outlined as follows.
  I. David's Administration (27:1-34)
    A. David's military arrangements (27:1-24)
    B. Stewards of the king's property (27:25-31)
    C. The king's associates (27:31-34)
 II. David's Final Arrangements (28:1–29:25)
    A. David's farewell to the leaders (28:1-8)
    B. David's advice to Solomon (28:9-10)
    C. Details of the temple plan (28:11-19)
    D. David's encouragement of Solomon (28:20-21)
    E. David's appeal to Israel's leaders (29:1-9)
    F. David's prayer (29:10-19)
    G. Celebration (29:20-22)
    H. Solomon's anointing as king (29:23-25)
III. David's Death (29:26-30)

David's Military Arrangements (27:1-24)

The ideal of an orderly military administration is attributed to David. The list of *officers who served the king*, army unit commanders, is taken from the list of David's early war heroes (chapter 11).

Thousands and hundreds are military units (Deuteronomy 1:15). There are twelve divisions (verses 2-15), each to be on active duty one month each year, and in this rotation system the nation can have a citizen's army of twenty-four thousand men in military readiness at all times.

Verses 16-22 list the *leaders* (commanding officers) *of the tribes of Israel* appointed by David over each of the tribes, omitting the tribes of Asher and Gad. Someone has written in *for Aaron, Zadok*, making a separate command for the priests (verse 17). In this way there are potential tribal army units posted throughout Israel. The list is associated with the military census (chapter 21), which was condemned. Even so, David numbered only those fit for military service. To have numbered those under twenty would have shown a lack of trust in God's promise that the people of Israel would be *as numerous as the stars of heaven* (verse 23; Genesis 15:5; 22:17).

Stewards of the King's Property (27:25-31)

Most heads-of-state own large properties. David's are diversified. From his properties, rather than from taxes, he acquires his wealth. David's stewards have responsibility for the management of his properties and for their produce. Scattered through the country, they are protected by watch towers. *The Shephelah*, foothills west of Jerusalem, and *Sharon*, a coastal plain, have reputations for their fertility.

The King's Associates (27:31-34)

A list of David's official cabinet appears in 18:15-17. Stories of most of these close associates of David appear in 1 and 2 Samuel. *Jonathan* (not the friend of David's youth who was killed in battle before David's reign) is renowned for his intelligence: *a man of understanding,* a trusted personal secretary (*scribe*). He, along with *Jehiel,* attended *the king's sons* as tutors. *The king's friend* is a title for one who, as an advisor with intimate knowledge of the king's mind, holds a position of considerable authority and responsibility. *Hushai* holds this position. *Jehoiada* and *Abiathar* succeeded *Ahithophel* when the latter defected to Absalom after that prince rebelled against his father (see the story in 2 Samuel 16:15–17:23). *Joab*'s name is repeated from verse 24.

David's Farewell to the Leaders (28:1-8)

David demonstrates complete faith in God and trust in the loyalty of Israel. The speech represents the Chronicler's basic message. David assembles all the leaders (as outlined in chapter 27) of *all Israel* (verse 4). He addresses them as *my brothers and my people.* Thus, he identifies with them and enjoins their participation. He prepares them for Solomon's role as king and builder of the temple. The emphasis is on the temple, a house *of rest for the ark of the covenant.* The temple is God's *footstool* (Psalm 132:7). David wanted to build it (chapter 17), but God would not permit it (chapter 22).

Solomon will be king not by human choice or by heredity, but because God has chosen him (verse 5). He will *establish his kingdom for ever,* yet conditionally: if he continues resolute in keeping my commandments. Here is the point of David's address: You must *seek* God's commandments (verse 8). To seek God is the religion of the Old Testament (Deuteronomy 4:29; Isaiah 55:6; Jeremiah 29:13). Psalm 119:2 could well express the pervading passion of the Chronicler: *Blessed are those . . . who seek him with their whole heart.* Only in seeking God's way can people be good stewards of the land and pass it on as a heritage to posterity.

David's Advice to Solomon (28:9-10)

David turns to Solomon to advise him publicly as he has done privately (22:6-16). The emphatic *seek* again appears: Seek God and *he will be found by you* (see Matthew 7:7). But the opposite is also true: *forsake* God and *he will reject you* (NIV; NRSV = *abandon*). There is responsibility in being chosen. The Lord searches and knows our inner thoughts. The advice ends in typical David style: encouragement to action.

Through David, the Chronicler is telling his contemporary readers that God is to be served joyfully and wholeheartedly.

Details of the Temple Plan (28:11-19)

David has already worked out plans for the temple and now gives them to Solomon. The Hebrew word for *plan* is the word translated *pattern* in God's instruction to Moses about the tent of meeting (Exodus 25:9, 40). The implication is that the plan David has in mind (verse 12) came to him by revelation from God.

The details for the vessels and furnishings to be made for the tabernacle and for the ark are given in Exodus 25. Thus the Chronicler shows the continuity between the tent of meeting set up by Moses and the temple to be built. *The division of the priests and of the Levites* (chapters 24 and 26) is related to these plans (verse 13).

David's Encouragement of Solomon (28:20-21)

This is the third time David encourages Solomon (22:11-13; 28:10). These verses also suggest, for the third time, David's anxiety about Solomon's ability to carry out the project. So he says, first trust in God (verse 20), and then see all these people who are willing and ready to help you (verse 21).

The first part has four elements: (1) *Be strong and of good courage* (22:13; 28:10; also Joshua 1:18); (2) don't be timorous; (3) *God is with you*; and (4) God *will not fail you or forsake you* as you build the temple. This assurance has helped many who commit themselves to God's service.

David's Appeal to Israel's Leaders (29:1-9)

Again David speaks *to the whole assembly*. He is going to make a strong appeal to them. These are his points: God has chosen Solomon to be king, to build the temple. Forget the other claimants to the throne (whose struggles are recorded in 2 Samuel and 1 Kings, but are ignored by the Chronicler). Solomon is young and inexperienced, but I count on you to help him. This is going to be a costly project. It is no ordinary royal palace, but a palace for God. I have done all I could; I have gathered all the materials, and gold and silver and gems. Beyond that, I have poured out all my treasures for the project because of my devotion to my God. (If David did not exaggerate what he gave, the Chronicler did: a quantity beyond imagination! Because one talent was about a seventy-five pound weight, just a few talents would make a person very rich.) Now what about you? Who among you will offer himself to the Lord? David appeals for both gift and giver.

Verses 6-9 show how profoundly successful is David's appeal. And because it is successful, there is much rejoicing. This story parallels the story that initiated the building of the tent of meeting (Exodus 25:1-7).

A *daric* is a standard coin minted under the Persian emperor, Darius (522–486 B.C.), long after David. For centuries, gold was mined in and exported from *Ophir* on the Red Sea coast.

David's Prayer (29:10-19)

Again all the assembly is present. The prayer begins with a doxology (verses 10-13). The anchor of the Chronicler's faith is the greatness, the power, and the eternal rule of God. God rules over all. All good comes from God. David prays with wonder and joy that God has chosen and blessed Israel. The phrasing is typical of Israel (see Daniel 2:20-23) and of the Psalms selected for worship before the ark (chapter 16). Praise and thanksgiving make up the framework in which the prayer is set. Humility and joy are the attitudes of David's prayer (verse 14). The kingdom is God's. All we have is God's. Everything in heaven and earth is God's. Whatever we have from God is for a little while, even our lives, for we are only temporary *aliens* on this earth (verse 15 and Psalm 39:12). David's prayer is remarkable in that after praise comes no request for himself.

Petitions for the people come briefly at the end of the prayer: May they love and serve God *freely* and *joyously* (verse 17). May their hearts be directed toward God (verse 18).

The prayer closes asking that Solomon be faithful to God's law (only thus can his family continue to rule Israel), and successfully complete the temple (God's *palace*).

For the Chronicler, seeking God and doing God's will must be with a whole heart (verse 19; see also 28:9; 29:9).

Celebration (29:20-22*a*)

David, having made a final prayer, leads all the assembly in worship that begins a two-day celebration. The worship begins with a response to David's call to bless God as a response to God who has chosen them. They respond by bowing their heads and worshiping. They prostrate themselves, a sign of submission to the king, who is an instrument of the Lord. The *sacrifices* are peace offerings, in which worshipers eat a portion of the ritually sacrificed animals, a kind of communion meal with God.

The next day there are *burnt offerings,* all consumed on the altar, and *drink offerings* (NIV; NRSV = *libations*) poured out. Eating and drinking together are both a celebration of joy and an experience of solidarity (12:39-40).

Solomon's Anointing as King (29:22*b*-25)

The second time must refer to 23:1, which is actually a caption for chapters 23–29. Solomon is anointed *prince* (NRSV; NIV = *ruler*), to be above his brothers who *pledged their allegiance* to him (verses 22, 24). This is essential to avoid fraternal rebellion (1 Kings 2:35). A note is added that *Zadok,* already serving as David's high priest (16:39), is anointed before all Israel to the high priest's office. The Lord makes Solomon great. This passage recalls the installation of Joshua (Joshua 1:16-18; 3:7).

David's Death (29:26-30)

The story of David is finished, but not before the story of Solomon has begun. Chapters 22–29 prepare the reader to see the continuity of David and Solomon with reference to the temple and to the splendor of God's kingdom in both their reigns.

David reigns over *all Israel* (verse 26). The Chronicler omits the fact that there was a long war between David and Saul before David reigned over all Israel (2 Samuel 3:1). It is enough for the Chronicler that God's purpose is for David to rule over all Israel.

Hebron in southern Judah was David's capital until he captured Jerusalem (11:1-9). The reference to the chronicles of David's three *seers* (religious advisers) may allude to their appearance in 1 and 2 Samuel and 1 and 2 Kings. *All the kingdoms of all the other lands* (NIV; NRSV = *of the earth*) are Israel's neighboring nations.

§ § § § § § §

The Message of 1 Chronicles 27–29

In chapter 27 the Chronicler depicts an orderly, stable society. In chapters 28 and 29 he gives David's public statement of faith in God's greatness, power, glory, victory, and majesty, and his confidence in a people who are faithful to God. He charges his son, Solomon, and the people to carry out his plans for a great temple for the worship of God. Consecrating their gifts and themselves to God, the people have great joy.

The message to the people of God is:

§ Let your house be in order. Manage responsibly what is entrusted to you.

§ Recognize the brevity and finiteness of life and that the rule of God, whom your spiritual ancestors worshiped, is over all creation forever.

§ Recognize that all you have is from God and belongs to God. Consecrate it to God, using it and your life, as faithful stewards, for the glory of God.

§ Follow responsibly the vocation God has given you.

§ In humility and joy, praise God's greatness, power, and glory, with thanksgiving for God's goodness.

§ Worship and celebrate God faithfully and publicly.

§ Seek God, study God's word, and understand and obey the commandments.

§ Serve God wholeheartedly, freely, and joyously.

§ Trust in God and live courageously. Let nothing dismay you or deter you from doing God's will persistently.

§ Let your motives and plans be pure in God's sight.

§ Do what you can to guide, inspire, and support others in their work for God.

§ Help those who do God's work and accept their help.

§ § § § § § §

PART EIGHT 2 Chronicles 1:1–5:1

Introduction to These Chapters

The first four chapters of 2 Chronicles detail the building and the structure of the Temple. Brief attention is given to Solomon's other public works, his wisdom, and his wealth.

Here is an outline of these chapters.
  I. Solomon's Reign Initiated with Worship (1:1-6)
  II. Solomon's Worship and God's Promise (1:7-13)
  III. God's Blessing on Solomon (1:14-17)
  IV. Preparations to Build the Temple (2:1–3:2)
  V. The Temple Measurements and Description (3:3–5:1)
      A. The Temple and nave (3:3-7)
      B. The Most Holy Place (3:8-14)
      C. The pillars (3:15-17)
      D. More Temple furnishings (4:1-22)
  VI. The Temple Finished (5:1)

Solomon's Reign Initiated with Worship (1:1-6)

Verse 1 is a heading for chapters 1–9. It is God who makes Solomon great because *the* LORD *his God was with him*. Solomon is not great in and of himself. His reign is inaugurated with a great religious ceremony at a famous shrine at Gibeon, north of Jerusalem. The Chronicler recognizes Moses' *tent of meeting* as the only authentic worship center until it is superseded by the Temple.

The tent of meeting was the portable gathering place

and worship center for the Israelites during their life in the desert prior to settling in Canaan. The Chronicler explains that the shrine in Gibeon, *the high place,* is the setting for this tent of meeting. The *ark,* the box representing God's presence, which had been in the tent of meeting, was brought to Jerusalem by David (1 Chronicles 13; 15:25-29).

The bronze altar is reputed to be the one made in the time of Moses (Exodus 31:1-9). Solomon with *all Israel,* represented by military, judicial, and other leaders, seeks God's blessing. Solomon's *thousand burnt offerings* may seem exaggerated, but the magnificence and quantity of a king's inaugural sacrifices were supposed to reflect the importance and wealth of the king and the effective power in his sacrifice.

Solomon's Worship and God's Promise (1:7-13)

Solomon *inquired* of God (verse 5) and God responds, asking Solomon what he wants (verse 7). Universal in early religion is the belief that God (or a god) is attracted to sacrifices and worship, and in response asks the worshiper what he desires. Solomon does not ask for his own gratification (possessions, wealth, honor, or long life, the things that most people desire). God will grant these, however, because Solomon's request is for *wisdom and knowledge* to rule his people (verse 11).

God's Blessing on Solomon (1:14-17)

These lines briefly describe King Solomon's great wealth and the activity by which his merchants help accumulate that wealth. *Kue* (Cilicia) is in southeast Asia Minor. The *Shephelah* (NRSV; NIV = *foothills*) is a wooded pastureland on the lower slopes west of the hill country in Judah.

Preparations to Build the Temple (2:1–3:2)

Now to the real business: *a temple for the name of the* LORD. The temple must be great and wonderful (verse 9).

The call to *Huram the king of Tyre* for help is careful to point out that the temple is for the worship of God, and is not intended to contain God. Although this is typical early oriental boasting, the words reflect the Chronicler's insistence on God's greatness that requires appropriate humility of kings: *Who am I to build a house for him?*

The amount of materials and the size of the work force seem excessive. *Huram* (*Hiram* in 1 Chronicles 14:1) is looked upon as a satellite of Solomon in Phoenicia, famed for its trees and its skilled workers. The sacrificial offerings Solomon mentions (verse 4) are prescribed in Numbers 28–29.

Huram's formal but complimentary reply enforces the Chronicler's theme that *the* LORD *has made you king over his people*. Huram will send the talented craftsman, Huramabi, a half-Israelite. When Solomon has sent the wages in kind that he has promised, Huram will send timber *in rafts* down the seacoast to Joppa, the nearest good port to Jerusalem. Solomon will transport the timber from there.

Verse 18 repeats the figures in verse 2. Aliens, though they may be largely Canaanites who lived in the land before the Israelite invasion, were considered sojourners, liable to slavery (Leviticus 25:39-55) and subject to periods of forced labor. (Herod's Temple, centuries later, was also built by forced labor.)

The location for the temple (now occupied by the Mosque of Omar) was selected by David by divine direction (1 Chronicles 21:18–22:1), and is the traditional site of Abraham's offer to sacrifice Isaac (Genesis 22:9). Temple construction begins in the *second month,* in the spring of the year.

The Temple and Nave (3:3-7)

Verses 3-7 give the general plan for the Temple. Although patterned after the tent of meeting of Moses (Exodus 26), the measurements are Solomon's. The Chronicler outdoes his sources in describing the splendor of the Temple. *Gold of Parvaim* is probably a phrase to describe the finest gold in the world (or Parvaim may have been Ophir—see 1 Chronicles 29:4). The *nave* (NRSV; NIV = *main hall*) is the larger of the two rooms of the Temple. It is also called the Holy Place and is restricted to priests.

Cherubim: see the note below on verse 10.

The Most Holy Place (3:8-14)

The most holy place is the square room at the end of the Temple, restricted from all human entry except that of the high priest once a year on the Day of Atonement (Leviticus 16; 23:27-28). *The upper chambers* (NRSV; NIV = *upper parts*): 1 Kings 6:5-10 says there were three stories to the Temple. Being forbidden to make images of any living creature (Exodus 20:4), the Israelites make a figure and carvings of symbolic creatures called *cherubim* (Exodus 25:18-20). The cherubim, like similar symbols in neighboring nations, express power. These symbols are placed so as to protect the ark. They probably had stylized lion bodies, human heads, and widespread wings—in this case very wide, about seven and one-half feet each. The *curtain* is a curtain that separates the Most Holy Place from the nave of the Temple (Exodus 26:31, 33).

The Pillars (3:15-17)

In front of the temple (NIV; NRSV = *house*) means at the entrance to the Holy Place (the nave). *Thirty-five cubits* means over fifty-two feet high (eighteen cubits according to 1 Kings 7:15.) The *pomegranate* fruit symbolizes fertility and prosperity. The names of the pillars are *Jachin* (*he established*) and *Boaz* (*in strength*).

More Temple Furnishings (4:1-22)

The tent of meeting and its furnishings were used as a model for the Temple. Details are found in Exodus 25–27 and 30–31.

Verses 1-6 are parallel to 1 Kings 7:23-26. Only such a

large *altar of bronze*, about 900 square feet, could hold the large quantities of animals sacrificed on it. *The molten sea* is for the priests to wash in. *The basins* are for the priests to rinse off what is used for the burnt offering. *Gourds* may be oxen shapes. *Baths* each contain about five and one-half gallons.

Verses 7-9 compare somewhat with 1 Kings 7:37-39, 48-49. The *golden lampstands* are described in Exodus 25:31-39. The *ten tables* are, presumably, to set the candlesticks on. The Temple courts are like those in Ezekiel's vision of the Temple (Ezekiel 40–48). *The great* (NRSV; NIV = *large*) *court* is for lay worshipers. From here they observe what goes on in front of the Temple and, when led by singers, they praise God here.

Verses 11-22 parallel 1 Kings 7:39-50, repeating some information already given, with some slight contradictions (the pillar capitals in 3:16 and 4:12, for example), and including some information omitted from previous verses.

Tables (verse 19)—only one would be in use—are for the bread of the Presence, twelve freshly-baked small loaves like those presented to honored guests or before a king. They are arranged on the table each sabbath, replacing those of the previous week (Exodus 25:30; see 1 Chronicles 9:32). The table is placed in the sanctuary just outside the Most Holy Place.

The Temple Finished (5:1)

The building *was finished* (5:1). Now the worship of the Lord in the Temple will begin and continue. This is the climax of the Chronicles; everything to this point was preparation. From now on the Chronicles will be concerned with observation—observation of worship and the law, or the failure to observe, with inevitable consequences. *The things his father David had dedicated* are from spoils of war and gifts (see 1 Chronicles 18:8, 10-11; 22:14; 26:26; 29:2-5).

The Message of 2 Chronicles 1:1–5:1

From Solomon's construction of the Temple the Chronicler draws a lesson for his times.

§ Solomon's reign was an ideal for Israel, growing as it did out of David's glorious reign.

§ Solomon, like his father, David, was God's instrument for the benefit of God's people.

§ What Solomon did was because of God's blessing.

§ God is too great to be localized in the Temple.

§ The place for all interest, all honor, all care, and all lavishing of gifts is the Temple of the Lord (nothing else is worth recording).

The message of this passage remains:

§ Look only to the best in the past as a pattern for the present.

§ Never look to a leader, or to any person, as the ultimate for your life; reserve that place for God.

§ Any good that human beings do, they do as an instrument of God's purpose, and such persons are to be esteemed only as long as they carry out God's purpose.

§ God chooses and uses persons on behalf of the chosen people, and never for themselves.

§ No one can do good except by God's blessing.

§ It is impossible to contain God in a definition, formula, description, or conceptualization of the human mind. God is greater than the universe, and so is greater than anything human beings can create.

§ The focus of all our interest, honor, care, time, gifts, and abilities must be that which glorifies God. The worship of God cannot be a sideline; it must be the mainline of our lives.

§ § § § § § §

2 Chronicles 5–7

Introduction to These Chapters

The summit of the Chronicles is reached in this passage. First Chronicles 1–9 was the approach: the generations from Adam to David. The story of David was the ascent to the summit: David's bringing the ark of the covenant of the Lord to Jerusalem and making everything ready for building a magnificent Temple in which to house it. Even Solomon's building of the temple was preparation for the great event: worship in the Temple. That is what these chapters are about.

Here is an outline of these chapters.
  I. The Ark of the Covenant to the Temple (5:1–6:1)
 II. Solomon's Prayer of Dedication (6:2-42)
III. The Closing Ceremonies (7:1-11)
 IV. God's Reply to Solomon's Prayer (7:12-22)

The Ark of the Covenant to the Temple (5:1–6:1)

The building is *finished* (verse 1). It is ready for the Lord. It is ready for the ark of the covenant that represents the presence of God among the people. Now the worship of the Lord in the Temple will begin, to be continued forever. This chapter (parallel to 1 Kings 8:1-66) carries on the Chronicler's assurance that the Temple is in continuity with the tent of meeting set up by Moses during the Exodus from Egypt.

As throughout the Chronicles, the king's proclamations are made before the leaders or *elders*, who represent Israel.

Solomon's assembly differs from David's in that military leaders are not mentioned (verses 2-3). The feast of the *seventh month* is the autumn feast of Tabernacles (Booths), celebrating Israel's crossing the wilderness and renewal of the covenant with God (Leviticus 23:34). They come to bring up the ark from *Zion*, the hill on which David's original Jerusalem was situated (1 Chronicles 11:4-7), and to which he had brought the ark (1 Chronicles 13–16).

The congregation (NRSV; NIV = *assembly*) *of Israel . . . before the ark* (verse 6) is a phrase used to recall their oneness as a people crossing the wilderness. The sacrifices were of epic proportions. The priests bring the ark, for only the priests are allowed inside the Temple. The ark is permanently lodged under the protective *wings of the cherubim*, which are described in 3:10-14. *The poles* are used to carry the ark. The *two tables* (verse 10) are the tables of stone engraved with the Ten Commandments (Exodus 24:12). *Horeb* is Mount Sinai, where the Ten Commandments were given to Moses (Exodus 19:16-20). The priests *had sanctified* (NRSV; NIV = *consecrated*) *themselves*, a ritual washing prescribed in the Mosaic law. *Asaph, Heman and Jeduthun:* These three, mentioned as leading singers at David's festivities, are three family guilds of singers who will be known by these names through the rest of the Chronicles.

Praise and thanksgiving to the Lord is always the emphasis in the Chronicler's account, never supplication. Musical instruments, singing, and the great assembly evoke a sound picture of joyful celebration. The *cloud* symbolizes the glory of God. It *filled the temple*, as in Exodus 40:34-35. God remains invisible in the thick darkness in the cloud (Exodus 20:21), and in the windowless Most Holy Place that Solomon has built.

Solomon's Prayer of Dedication (6:2-42)

Solomon addresses the assembled people by summing up the significance of the Temple: It represents God's covenant with Israel. It is the fulfillment of God's choice of Israel, of Jerusalem, and of David and Solomon. It is the fulfillment of God's promise (verses 4 and 10).

Solomon prays kneeling, with his hands spread to heaven (like the prayer recorded in 1 Kings 8:22-53). He prays on a platform in full public view, because the king's prayer is a speaking to God on behalf of his people. Praise of God is followed by an indirect appeal to Israel and a comment on history: that all the kings of David's dynasty should walk in the law.

In verse 18, the Chronicler includes in Solomon's prayer the unique mystery of the Hebrew (and so also Christian) faith: wonder at the immeasurable greatness of God who nevertheless can dwell with us. The focus here (verses 19-21) is the Temple, as Israel's place of prayer which is close to God, whose real dwelling place is heaven.

Verses 22-39 are petitions that are also to the people, and undoubtedly applicable to the people of the Chronicler's day. All social and natural problems can have their solution at the altar of God: justice between individuals (verses 22-23), the restoration to their land if they are exiled in war (verses 24-25, 36-39), rain in time of drought (verses 26-27), forgiveness for any wrongdoing that has brought about calamity (verses 28-31), and acceptance of and blessing on all foreigners who worship God in Israel (verses 32-33). Against the movement of some for a narrow nationalistic Judaism, the Chronicler follows the great prophets who saw Israel as God's witness to the nations that *all the peoples of the earth may know your name and fear you, as do your people Israel* (verse 33).

Support in war is asked for, if the war is engaged in by people who follow God's direction (verse 34).

All prayers are made facing in the direction of Jerusalem and its Temple (verse 34). All the prayers restate the Chronicler's belief that good (righteousness) is rewarded and evil punished. All the petitions conclude with the necessity of faithfulness to God and the law. They call for total repentance (verse 38).

Two words form a foundation for the prayers: *covenant* and *promise*. God is a covenant-keeping God. The covenant, or contract, with Israel is attested to in the Ten Commandments, which are kept in the ark of the covenant. God's promise was made to David, that his descendants would rule in Israel. God's promise is sure, yet conditioned on human faithfulness (verses 24, 36). The prayer is a litany in which each petition is followed by such phrases as *hear from heaven* (God's dwelling place) *and forgive* (verses 25, 29), and *maintain their cause* (verses 35, 39). Also repeated is the counsel to walk before the Lord, which is to live openly in God's presence. God is not confined to the Temple, but prayers are to be made *toward this house* (the Temple). Then people are to pray *with all their heart*. Sincerity is essential.

The prayer closes with a request for God's response, an invitation to God to enter the Temple, and a request for the priests and the saints. God's people are the saints. Verses 41-42 echo Psalm 132:8-10.

The Closing Ceremonies (7:1-11)

This passage parallels 1 Kings 8:54–9:1. The dedication is confirmed dramatically by fire from heaven, by the glory of the Lord's presence, and by the rejoicing of the throng of people. As the fire consumes the huge sacrifice (5:6), *the glory of the Lord filled the temple* (as before in 5:14), both inside where the priests have deposited the ark of the covenant, and outside on the Temple, so that all the people can see. They respond with praise. The theme of their praise is God's steadfast love for the people, a phrase that is most characteristic of the psalm that the Levites sing.

The priests, the Levites, and all the people make up the *vast assembly* (NIV; NRSV = *great congregation*) that extends from the entrance of Hamath, in the north of Israel, *to the Wadi of Egypt* in the south. They celebrate with music. For music's place in worship, the Chronicler

1 AND 2 CHRONICLES

credits David. *A solemn assembly* closes the feast of Tabernacles, which follows the dedication, on the eighth day (Leviticus 23:34-36).

God's Reply to Solomon's Prayer (7:12-22)

This passage, a parallel to 1 Kings 9:2-9, records a second divine affirmation. After the crowd has dispersed, God appears to Solomon in the night (as in 1:7-12) in answer to his prayer. It is a poetic response in that it matches the phrases of the prayer. It begins with God's assertion: I *have chosen* the Temple (verses 12, 16). That takes the initiative away from Solomon, whose building of the Temple is now recognized as a participation in God's promise to David (1 Chronicles 17:11-14). Verses 14 and 20 respond to 6:20. The seriousness of God's decision will be underscored in chapter 33.

In response to Solomon's concern for his people, God names three possible problems: drought, devastation from locusts, and pestilence. God will forgive and heal. The phrase *if my people* corresponds to *if your people* in the prayer.

Verses 14 and 19-20 become the measure by which all the kings and people of Judah will be judged. God *will hear from heaven* (a phrase also found in the prayer) as the consequence of their faithfulness. They must humbly seek God's face (a frequent exhortation in the Chronicles) and *turn from their wicked ways* (verse 14), a plea that is found in the prophets (see, for example, Isaiah 55:6-7). Verse 15 is a response to the prayer in 6:40 (and 6:20) for God to have open eyes and attentive ears.

Verses 16-18 respond to Solomon's concern about the king's relationship to God. The dynasty will continue.

There is also a consequence of faithlessness, however. *Forsake* is the Chronicler's contrasting word to *seek*. The people seek God and the commandments, or they forsake them. If they forsake them, God's response is to *pluck you up* (NRSV; NIV = *uproot you*) *from the land I have given you* which, the Chronicler knows, is what happened in 586 B.C. (see 1 Chronicles 9:1).

§ § § § § § §

The Message of 2 Chronicles 5–7

This section of 2 Chronicles is about the celebration when the ark of the covenant is brought and lodged in the newly built, magnificent Temple. Both Solomon's dedicatory prayer and God's response carry counsel that emphasize the relationship of Israel and Israel's king with God. The key words are *seek* and *forsake*. If you do not seek, you are forsaking God. If you do not forsake God, it is because you are seeking God. The message for all times is:

§ Set aside a place and time for prayer and praise as a covenant people.

§ Worship in the congregation with music and joy.

§ God's presence is not to be taken lightly, but with profound awe and a sincere heart.

§ Live openly before God, who knows all our thoughts and motives.

§ Interpersonal and intergroup problems can be solved at the altar of God, as can all political, civil, and physical problems.

§ At the altar, forgiveness for wrongdoing can be received.

§ Pray for faithfulness to God and obedience to the law.

§ Invite God into your life and expect a response.

§ Tune your life to God's presence so that you may be a living witness for God to all people.

§ § § § § § §

2 Chronicles 8–9

Introduction to These Chapters

Solomon's fame, his building and taking of cities, his cities of stone houses, his chariots and horsemen, his wealth, his merchandising and importing on Phoenician ships, fetching great quantities of gold, his enslavement of non-Israelite people for building projects, his complete internal control of the land, the amazement at his wisdom and wealth (shown by the Queen of Sheba and by neighboring kings), his pageantry, prosperity, his brilliant court, the constant scent of sacrifices at his great Temple: All these the Chronicler records in order to picture a fame and respect such as Israel has never known before and will never know again in its long history.

Solomon's glory is a reflection of his having built the Temple. The Temple is evidence that he truly honors and worships God and obeys the commandments. Solomon, Jerusalem, and Israel, like David, are rewarded for putting God and righteousness first.

Here is an outline of these chapters.
I. Solomon, Builder and Despot (8:1-10)
II. Temple Worship (8:11-16)
III. Greatness of Solomon (8:17–9:31)
    A. Solomon's enterprise (8:17-18)
    B. Queen of Sheba (9:1-12)
    C. Solomon's wealth (9:13-21)
    D. Solomon's wealth, wisdom, and power (9:22-28)
IV. Solomon's End (9:29-31)

Solomon, Builder and Despot (8:1-10)

The house of God was Solomon's first business. He spent about seven years building the Temple. All else he did was secondary, but considerable. *The cities that Huram had given to him* reverses the account in 1 Kings 9:10-14, which says that Solomon gave Hiram (the Huram of Chronicles) twenty cities.

The Kings account permits the interpretation that Solomon had given these cities, on the edge of his kingdom and nearer to Tyre than to Jerusalem, to Hiram in payment for his contributions toward building the Temple and his own palace (2:3-16). Furthermore, the 1 Kings account says that Hiram was displeased with them. Reading 2 Chronicles after Kings, one could surmise that Solomon then improved these cities that Hiram had given back by building walls around them. At any rate, the Chronicler's main interest is to show Solomon's power, wealth, and order. He settled the people of Israel in these cities as an imperial policy, thus anchoring the outskirts of his kingdom with his own people.

Verses 3-6 parallel 1 Kings 9:17-19. *Hamath-zobah* (verse 3) is in the extreme north of Israel, east of Mount Lebanon. *Tadmor* (verse 4) is probably modern Palmyra southwest of the Dead Sea (*Tamar* in the 1 Kings passage). Thus Solomon secures the outer reaches of the kingdom. *Upper Beth-horon and Lower Beth-horon* (verse 5) are militarily strategic towns near Gibeon, northwest of Jerusalem. They serve as defense points. *Baalath* will guard his western defenses deep in land taken from Philistines.

Verses 7-11 parallel 1 Kings 9:20-23. They show Solomon as a rich and powerful despot, with wealth enough to build cities and his own treasure-house, and power enough to order the lives of his people, Israel. They accept his rule because the economy is good, and they, the Israelites, are exempted from labor on the king's projects. *Forced* labor is performed by levies of *Hittites,*

Amorites, Perizzites, Hevites, and *Jebusites* (verse 7) who are descended from earlier inhabitants left after the Israelites invaded and took the land (verse 8). The people of Israel are not used by Solomon as slaves, but as soldiers, army leaders, overseers of his work projects, buyers and importers, and even sailors. Despite this and the nation's prosperity, the taxes are high and the service hard, and the Israelites become restive, according to 1 Kings 12:4. Solomon's *two hundred and fifty,* who exercised authority over the people (verse 10) indicates that Solomon's rule is direct, through his personally chosen representatives throughout the land, and that an earlier, more democratic system of the old tribal confederacy no longer prevails.

Temple Worship (8:11-16)

Pharaoh's daughter (1 Kings 9:24) is the only wife of Solomon mentioned by the Chronicler. She is mentioned only with reference to the Temple worship. Because the ark of the covenant has been brought to the newly built Temple, it is too close to the pagan princess. Its sacred power makes the place near it *holy.* It is taboo, or dangerous to unholiness (see 1 Chronicles 13:9-10). No one apart from the priests, especially the high priest (and he only after ritual cleansing) is safe near such power, least of all a non-Israelite. For her own safety, the queen has to be moved to a new, more distant palace.

Verses 12-15 parallel 1 Kings 9:25. The Temple is built for the purpose of the perpetual worship of God (see 2:4). *Burnt offerings* (verse 12) are the most complete offerings, made on solemn occasions when the sacrificed victim is entirely burned on the altar (described in 4:1; see Numbers 28–29). The *three annual feasts* were (1) *the feast of Unleavened Bread,* a seven-day feast in the spring, connected with the Passover (Exodus 12:1–13:16), (2) seven weeks later, *the feast of Weeks,* a one-day wheat harvest festival (described in Deuteronomy 16:9-12), and

(3) *the feast of tabernacles* (or of booths), a seven-day harvest festival in autumn that celebrates Israel's wandering in the wilderness before settling in Canaan (described in Deuteronomy 16:13-15).

Verses 14-15, added by the Chronicler, refer to offices of the priests and Levites described in 1 Chronicles 26. *The duty of each day* (NRSV; NIV = *each day's requirement*) refers to the daily offerings. *The divisions of the priests* were set up by *the ordinance of David*, according to the Chronicler, although scholars believe that the practice was developed much later (see the explanation of the divisions in the comments on 1 Chronicles 24). The Chronicler emphasizes the importance of *the Levites*, the priests' assistants. The duties concerning *the treasuries* are described in 1 Chronicles 26:20-32.

Verse 16 is one of the Chronicler's frequent reminders that the Temple of the Lord is the theme of the story of Solomon (2:1; 5:1; 7:11; 8:1, 16).

Greatness of Solomon (8:17–9:31)

The last passages about Solomon are intended to record his greatness. His most profitable commerce seems to be with the lands bordering the Red Sea. The Queen of Sheba's visit is in association with this commerce. The report goes on to say that not only the Queen of Sheba but also many kings admire his wisdom, and that riches pour in from them all. Moreover, his influence is more widely extended than at any other time in Israel's history.

Solomon's Enterprise (8:17-18)

These verses parallel 1 Kings 9:26-28. *Ezion-geber,* which is near *Eloth,* is a port city at the head of the Gulf of Aqaba, an arm of the Red Sea. Merchant ships come and go from this port trading with *Ophir* (somewhere on the coast of the Red Sea), mostly for gold (see 1 Chronicles 29:4). Men of Israel go with Phoenician seamen in this trade for Solomon. This information is confirmed in 9:10-11.

Queen of Sheba (9:1-12)

These verses parallel 1 Kings 10:1-13. *Sheba* stands for the Sabaean people. Studies indicate that branches of these people existed in northwestern Arabia, in south Arabia, and possibly in a colony on the Ethiopian coast of the Red Sea. The southern branch was particularly engaged in trade. It has already been noted that Solomon was engaged in the trade of this area. Thus, it is clear that trade talks bring the desert queen, besides a desire to see the king so reputed for his wisdom.

Middle-eastern culture valued readiness of wit. People enjoyed gatherings for the exchange of riddles, the recitation of proverbs, and the telling of stories. Solomon apparently has a reputation for his ability at such gatherings (although Chronicles does not repeat the story of Solomon's additional reputation for judicial wisdom; see 1 Kings 3:16-28).

The house (NRSV; NIV = *palace*) *that he had built* (verse 3), which the Queen of Sheba saw, is probably the entire building project in Jerusalem that includes, as its crown, the Temple. Over the span of thirteen years, after building the Temple, Solomon has constructed a palace complex, including *the house (Palace) of the Forest of Lebanon* (verse 16), the hall of judgment, the king's royal quarters, and the palace for his Egyptian queen (8:11). The Chronicler, writing in a time of Israel's poverty, takes pride in the fame of Solomon's wealth (verses 3-4). All that the Queen of Sheba sees and hears takes her breath away (verse 4).

The queen sees great wealth, but it is Solomon's great wisdom that arouses her admiration (verse 6).

In quoting the queen, the Chronicler shows his emphasis on God in contrast to the same quotation in 1 Kings 10:9. For the Chronicler, the kingdom and the throne are God's. The king is God's instrument on behalf of God's people (see 1 Chronicles 17:14).

The *servants* (NRSV; NIV = *men) of Solomon* (verse 10) add to his importance along with the servants of Huram (see 1 Kings 10:11).

Algum wood (see 2:8) is probably a reddish sandalwood used for making instruments.

All that she desired: There was no trade imbalance unless in Israel's favor. The produce of Solomon's kingdom is sufficient to supply all the Queen of Sheba's requests and is more than she brought to Solomon. He exchanges, in other words, what is equal in value to what she brought him, and he adds even more. In Eastern thought, generosity is a sign of greatness.

Solomon's Wealth (9:13-21)

Verses 13-28 (corresponding to 1 Kings 10:14-29) underline the affluence of Solomon's Israel. He has great mining and smelting works. *Six hundred sixty-six*: If verse 14 refers to trade with Solomon, it almost sounds like tribute to the great king (see also verses 23-24).

The House (NRSV; NIV = *Palace) of the Forest of Lebanon* (verse 16) was built with wood from Lebanon (2:16). The *ivory throne* showed a magnificence that later Muslim emperors tried to imitate. The Chronicler boasts that such a throne *was never made in any other kingdom* (verse 19). The additional boasts in verses 20-24 are used to support the Chronicler's assurance that God blessed Solomon (1:12). Cedar (verse 27) is used because it is a strong building material, but it has to be imported.

The king's ships went to *Tarshish* (verse 21). Tarshish is a Mediterranean seaport (Jonah 1:3). *Ships of Tarshish*, however, may be all that the Chronicler means (1 Kings 10:22). *Ships of Tarshish* is a phrase applied to a type of ship equipped to carry cargo a long distance, making the round trip voyage once every three years.

Solomon's Wealth, Wisdom, and Power (9:22-28)

Solomon's wealth comes from commerce, mining, tribute, and gifts. Although the Chronicler boasts of Solomon's wealth, he notes especially that Solomon's contemporaries were greatly impressed with his wisdom. Most ancient civilizations had their heroes of wisdom and invention. Solomon was such a hero in Israel.

Archaeology has unearthed large stable complexes, such as the stables for 450 horses excavated at Megiddo in northern Israel. None have been found as large as Solomon's stables described in verse 25. No disapproval of Solomon (compare 1 Kings 11) is found in the Chronicler's account of the ideal Solomon, obedient to God's will as God's agent.

Solomon's End (9:29-31)

Verses 29-31 parallel 1 Kings 11:41-42. Either the histories of the *seers*, the king's religious advisers, *Nathan*, *Ahijah*, and *Iddo* were separate books or, because there is no sure evidence of source material not found in 1 and 2 Samuel or 1 and 2 Kings, the reference may simply be to source material in these books about Nathan (1 Kings 1), Ahijah (1 Kings 11:29-30), and Iddo (12:15; 13:22), who may have been the unnamed *man of God* in 1 Kings 13:1-10.

Solomon continues his father David's glorious reign for, the accounts say, an equally long time: *forty years* (verse 30).

§ § § § § § §

The Message of 2 Chronicles 8–9

This section of 2 Chronicles is a counsel to leaders of God's people and, by implication, to all of God's people to:

§ Make the first business of life whatever pertains to the worship of God.

§ Make the second business of life wisely, responsibly, and practically to administer whatever is under your charge.

§ Use all the resources available to you to carry out these responsibilities.

§ Maintain awe for the sacred.

§ Worship God faithfully in public worship.

§ Remember that what you do, what you say, and what you are show what is really important to you in life. No one is without a reputation. Let your reputation glorify God, not you.

§ Let God be foremost in your life.

§ Use for God what you receive.

§ Make God your point of reference.

§ Rejoice in the abundance of riches with which God has endowed this world.

To add New Testament perspective to this message:

§ Remember that God is Spirit, unbound to place or form, and so to be worshiped *in spirit and truth* (John 4:23).

§ Understand that life in Christ, who called his followers to forsake all they have, is not dependent on possessions nor expectant of physical rewards.

§ Worship as Jesus worshiped, for this will lead to a deep love for God and for all people.

§ § § § § § §

2 Chronicles 10–13

Introduction to These Chapters

Rehoboam inherits the wealth and power of his father, Solomon. He quickly squanders them by offending and turning the majority of the nation's tribes against him, and turning God against him by forsaking God's law. The first failure brings about invasion by the Egyptian king. Only repentance saves Rehoboam's kingdom. Abijah succeeds Rehoboam. Facing great odds in battle, he and his people rely on God and are victorious.

Here is an outline of these chapters.
I. The Division of the Kingdom (10:1–11:14)
   A. Rehoboam's response to the people (10:1-15)
   B. Separation of the northern tribes (10:16-19)
   C. Failure to quell the rebellion (11:1-4)
II. Rehoboam's Good Three Years (11:5-23)
   A. Rehoboam as military builder (11:5-12)
   B. Faithful Israelites in Jerusalem (11:13-17)
   C. Rehoboam's big family (11:18-23)
III. Egyptian Invasion of Judah (12:1-12)
IV. The End of Rehoboam (12:13-16)
V. The Reign of Abijah (13:1-22)
   A. Abijah's confrontation with Jeroboam (13:1-12)
   B. The battle (13:13-20)
   C. The rest of Abijah's reign (13:20-22)

Rehoboam's Response to the People (10:1-15)

Jeroboam has fled from King Solomon. The Chronicler omits the reason given in 1 Kings 11:26-36.

Your father made our yoke heavy. This circumstance is described in 1 Kings 5:13-14; 11:28, but is omitted by the Chronicler, who wishes to record only the best about Solomon. Solomon required *hard service* (NRSV; NIV = *labor*) in his ambitious military, building, mining, and merchandising projects, and heavy yoke in taxes. Despite Solomon's despotism, the people keep to their traditional tribal role of selecting their common leader.

If you will be kind to this people: This is wise and seasoned politicians' counsel. It does not, however, carry the king-servant concept as does the advice found in 1 Kings 12:7. *The young men* give their foolish advice *when Rehoboam was young and irresolute* (13:7 [NRSV; NIV = *indecisive*]). Their youthful boasting (verses 10-11) results from their growing up in an atmosphere of royal splendor with no appreciation for the democratic traditions of earlier generations.

An outcome brought about *by God* (verse 15) is due to Rehoboam's failure to be faithful to God. This refers to the words spoken to Jeroboam by Ahijah reported in 1 Kings 11:33, but not included by the Chronicler (see also 1 Kings 11:9-11). In a similar way God turned the kingdom over to David when King Saul proved to be unfaithful (1 Chronicles 10:14). Although the Chronicler does not wish to spell this out, he assumes knowledge of 1 Kings 11:29-40 by adding that *the LORD might fulfill his word, which he spoke by Ahijah* that Jeroboam should become king of the tribes torn away from Jerusalem.

Separation of the Northern Tribes (10:16-19)

What share do we have begins a folk verse, a war-cry of independence already used in the abortive rebellion against David reported in 2 Samuel 20:1. It is a declaration of independence from the dynasty of David. Although only the nine or ten breakaway tribes are meant here, the Chronicler uses *all Israel* to mean both the Northern Kingdom and the Southern Kingdom. So *Israel* (verse 19) means those who rebel against the house of David, and the people of Israel (verse 17) are those who remain loyal to David's house.

Failure to Quell the Rebellion (11:1-4)

The rebellion begins in violence with the assassination of Rehoboam's agent (10:18). Instead of sending a reconciler, Rehoboam sends a taskmaster whose approach is probably arrogant. Rehoboam, of course, tries to curb the rebellion. *Shemaiah the man of God*, speaking for God, forbids Rehoboam to fight against his *brothers*: Both sides are still God's people. This is God's doing (see the comment above on 10:15). Hence, to fight them would be to fight against God's will.

Rehoboam as Military Builder (11:5-12)

Kings in good standing with the Lord had building periods in their reigns, according to the Chronicler's account (see 8:1-12). Rehoboam *built cities for defense*. He fortifies cities in a half-perimeter: east, south, and west, with Jerusalem at the core. A look at the map of the period will show the location of these cities (listed in verses 6-11). Some were at important road and valley approaches into the hill country of Judah: *Bethlehem, Tekoa, Beth-zur, Adoraim, Ziph,* and *Hebron.* Farther out, in the lowlands, Rehoboam fortifies *Lachish* and *Gath.* (This Philistine city of Gath may have been an independent city-state in the time of Solomon.) These approaches would be those most likely used by an invading Egyptian army as possible allies to Jeroboam (10:2). No fortifications against Jeroboam's Israel are mentioned, as though Rehoboam still hopes for their return to his rule.

Faithful Israelites in Jerusalem (11:13-17)

Because Jeroboam abandons the worship of God, people in the Northern Kingdom *who had set their hearts* to seek the Lord God come to worship at the Temple in

Jerusalem. This strengthens the morale of Judah's kingdom. Jeroboam, according to 1 Kings 12:15-33, sets up substitute gods and shrines in Israel to keep his people from going to Jerusalem to worship. For these shrines he appoints priests who are not Levites, the traditional tribe of religious leaders. Unemployed and unrecognized, these Levites, who had been posted all over Israel (1 Chronicles 6:54-81), left their common lands and holdings and came to Judah and Jerusalem. From time to time the Chronicler will remind the readers of faithful Israelites who travel from the north to worship at Jerusalem.

Jeroboam sets up satyrs for worship, which are demons in the form of he-goats, whose worship is condemned in Leviticus 17:7.

Rehoboam's Big Family (11:18-23)

A large family (verse 21) is another sign of blessing. Rehoboam marries *Mahalath*, a second cousin. Her father, *Jerimoth*, is not listed among the sons of David in 1 Chronicles 3:1-9, so he may be the son of one of David's concubines. Rehoboam's favorite wife, *Maacah*, is a daughter of *Absalom* (also spelled Abishalom in 1 Kings 15:2), not necessarily David's son Absalom.

Royal descent was not always through the eldest son. Kings chose their successors from among their sons. As David chose Solomon, Rehoboam chooses Abijah to succeed him. He wisely prepares for an orderly succession (to avert the usual struggle between sons for the throne) by appointing his other sons to scattered posts, and providing them with many wives.

For three years Judah is faithful to God's law (verse 17). The Chronicler omits Solomon's unfaithfulness to God (1 Kings 12).

Egyptian Invasion of Judah (12:1-12)

Chronicles 12 parallels 1 Kings 14:21-31. According to the Chronicler, a king either seeks God or he forsakes

God. When Rehoboam is *established* and is *strong,* he forgets the source of his strength (11:17) and *he forsook the law of the* LORD and *all Israel* (Judah and Benjamin) *with him.* This statement assures the reader that the people, as well as the king, deserve punishment. The Chronicler believes that all the people should, ideally, be true to God's worship in Jerusalem (13:5; 24:5; 28:23; 29:24; 31:1).

Disaster comes, as it always does, because they had been unfaithful to the LORD. *Shishak king of Egypt* is a Libyan commander in Egypt's army who seized power in Egypt and established its twenty-second dynasty. An engraved pillar, which he set up at Megiddo (in northern Israel), and engravings on the Egyptian temple of Karnak record his version of the invasion (926 B.C., and *the fifth year of Rehoboam's reign*), by which he overruns not only Judah, stripping its Temple of treasure, but also northern Israel and many neighboring cities and states. This is the first time since the victories of David that any foreign power has considered Judah and Israel weak enough to be attacked. *Libyans* form the officer corps of the Egyptian army at this time. *Sukkiim* are an unknown tribe, who, according to an early Greek translation, are cave-dwellers. *Ethiopians* are mercenaries from south of Egypt. Some of *the fortified cities*, mentioned in 11:6-11, are also listed in Shishak's record of his conquests.

You abandoned me, so I have abandoned you (verse 5). This is the Chronicler's doctrine of reward and punishment. The princes of Judah repent in acknowledging the justice of God's abandoning them. As the Chronicler regularly notes, there is always hope because, through penitence, punishment can be minimized (verses 7-8). They will, however, learn the difference between being loyal *servants* to God and to *other lands,* meaning neighboring nations.

The fame and the treasure of Solomon's Temple (4:7-10, 19-22; 9:13-21) naturally arouse the cupidity of neighboring kings, so that when the king of Egypt feels strong enough and finds the divided Israel weak enough through civil war, he takes the treasure (verse 9). For the Chronicler this is the shame that comes upon Rehoboam for his apostasy. The reduction of Jerusalem's glory is marked by the pitiful account of Rehoboam substituting bronze for gold in the shields of the officers of the guard (verses 10-11). As Rehoboam submitted to the prophet Shemaiah's warning against fighting Jeroboam (11:1-4), now he accepts the reality of Egypt's invasion and humbles himself in order to avoid complete destruction. Conditions would not have been good in Judah if Shishak had leveled the cities and burned the countryside as conquerors passing through often did. Shishak spares Judah because, according to the Chronicler, the people and the king repent and reform.

The End of Rehoboam (12:13-16)

Because of his father's long reign, Rehoboam is *forty-one* when he inherits the throne. The supremacy of Jerusalem (see 6:6) is never lost sight of, no matter what happens. *He did not set his heart to seek the LORD*: That is Rehoboam's great tragedy. Chronicles was not written by *Shemaiah* (11:3) *the prophet* and *Iddo the seer* (9:29; 13:22), but from their religious point of view. The distinction between *prophet* and *seer* is not to be overdrawn, but the seer is more likely to be a person in the king's employ.

Abijah's Confrontation with Jeroboam (13:1-12)

In the eighteenth year of King Jeroboam: The Chronicler does not use the northern Israelite kings as points of reference. Jeroboam, however, is important in Abijah's story. The numbers in the armies seem more realistic if every *thousand* stands for a unit of much fewer men: Jeroboam, with twice as many men as Abijah, has eight hundred units of *picked mighty warriors* (NRSV; NIV = *able troops*) against four hundred units of Abijah's *picked men* (NRSV; NIV = *able fighting men*).

Abijah's harangue is designed to weaken the Israelite army's confidence and to invite them back to the true God and true king. It also furnishes background for understanding the split of the northern tribes. The speech is given from *Mount Zemaraim*. This may be at the town of the same name near Bethel in the southern hill country of Ephraim (northern Israel), near its border with Judah.

The true kings of Israel are the heirs of David, fixed by a *covenant of salt* with God (1 Chronicles 21; 2 Chronicles 6:42). When two parties agree to an unbreakable bond between them, it is customary to eat together. Then they can say, *There is salt between us.* The bond with God is an everlasting covenant (Leviticus 2:13). Jeroboam, therefore, is a false king who breaks the covenant and is trying to stand up to God. Now, he has nothing to rely on but *golden calves* and false priests of false gods instead of the divinely ordained priests and Levites. The contrast is vivid.

The Battle (13:13-20)

The priests blowing *trumpets* is a way of calling on God to give them victory, according to Numbers 10:8-9. There follows a great slaughter of the enemy, and the capture of towns near their southern border. The same Hebrew verb is used for *God defeated* (NRSV; NIV = *routed*) *Jeroboam* (verse 15) and God *struck him down* (verse 20).

The Rest of Abijah's Reign (13:20-22)

Jeroboam does not recover his power, but Abijah grows mighty. His large family is a sign of God's blessing. The story of the prophet Iddo has already been used as a reference (see 9:20; 12:15).

§ § § § § § §

The Message of 2 Chronicles 10–13

The stories of Rehoboam and Abijah show the good that goes with faithfulness to God, and the trouble that attends failure to obey. Rehoboam has success when he is true to God, but trouble when he forsakes God. Abijah triumphs over Jeroboam, the northern Israelite king, because Abijah's people rely on God, whereas Jeroboam and his people forsake God.

Aspects of this message can be applied today.

§ Listen to those who have complaints. Be kind to them.

§ Listen to wise and mature counsel; do not depend on the shallow counsel of your contemporaries.

§ Be conciliatory, not arrogant, in your dealings.

§ Do not enter into any struggle to assert yourself, but only follow God's direction.

§ Deal wisely with whatever is entrusted to you.

§ Do not go along with those who forsake their faith, but keep company with those who worship God.

§ Beware lest, when all seems well with you, you abandon God and neglect the law.

§ When you suffer from wrong you have done, humble yourself, accept God's punishment as your due, repent, and seek God.

§ In the conflicts and struggles of life, be sure of which side you are on. Do not be on the side of those who, in rebellion against God, rely on substitutes for God.

§ Whatever your strengths or weaknesses, put all your trust in the Lord, rely on God, and call to God for help.

§ § § § § § §

2 Chronicles 14–16

Introduction to These Chapters

This section narrates the reforms of King Asa, fifth king of Judah in the line of David. He tries to restore Judah to the worship of God and to destroy the worship of pagan gods. His peaceful reign is interrupted by an invading Ethiopian-Libyan army, but he is victorious because he and his people rely on the Lord. When Baasha, the king of Israel, wages war against Judah, Asa relies on the king of Syria instead of on the Lord. For this he is condemned, and is punished with illness.

Careful students of the accounts have suggested the following chronology of Asa's reign. During his first fifteen years he engages in reform. In his fifteenth year, Judah is invaded by *Zerah, the* Cushite (NIV; NRSV = *Ethiopian*). In his sixteenth year, he engages in war with Israel under King Baasha and makes a treaty with Ben-hadad, king of Syria.

Here is an outline of these chapters.
  I. King Asa's Reforms (14:1-8)
 II. The Ethiopian Invasion (14:9–15:19)
    A. Overwhelming the invaders (14:9-15)
    B. Azariah's sermon of encouragement (15:1-7)
    C. The covenant celebration (15:8-15)
    D. Asa's zeal for the house of the Lord (15:16-19)
 III. War with Baasha and Its Consequences (16:1-10)
    A. Border struggles with Israel (16:1-6)
    B. Hanani's sermon of condemnation (16:7-10)
 IV. Asa's End (16:11-14)

King Asa's Reforms (14:1-8)

The country was at peace (NIV; NRSV = *the land had rest* verses 1, 5-7). *Peace* is the result of Asa's obedience to God. *Rest* is God's promise to the people as a hope and reward (Exodus 33:14). Verse 3 shows the prevalence of Canaanite religion, which Hebrew law condemns (Deuteronomy 7:5). It is *foreign* to Hebrew faith. To seek the Lord (the major admonition throughout Chronicles) always includes the need to *keep the law and the commandment*. The Lord is clearly distinguished from any other gods of the land by being identified as *the God of their fathers* (NIV; NRSV = *ancestors*).

High places were built for worship of idols and, frequently, for human sacrifices throughout the ancient Near East. Hebrew law always condemns them (Numbers 33:52). *Incense altars* are shrines. *Let us build these cities*: The reward to righteous kings is peace and the opportunity to build (see the comment on 11:5). *The land is still ours,* because at the time the Chronicler wrote, the land was no longer theirs. It was under foreign control because of Judah's apostasy (1 Chronicles 9:1).

Asa's army is larger than Abijah's had been (400,000). The army figures seem impossibly large. *Thousands* may be a general figure for army units.

Overwhelming the Invaders (14:9-15)

Judah is invaded in the fifteenth year of Asa's reign (15:10-11). The immense army, utterly defeated by the much smaller army of Judah, is evidence of God's protection of the righteous. *Ethiopian* (NRSV) is a biblical designation not of modern Ethiopia, but of Cush, a land south of Egypt on the Upper Nile. According to 16:8, it is an Ethiopian-Libyan army. Scholars have suggested that the actual event is the encroachment into Judah of a Bedouin tribe or possibly an Egyptian contingent near southern Judah. *A million men* is a round figure for a huge number, a large force outnumbering the army of

Judah. *Mareshah* is a fortified town near the southwestern borders of Judah in the Shephelah, the foothills sloping down to Judah's western borders. This would be a likely approach for invaders. *Zephathah* may mean *just north of Mareshah*.

Azariah's Sermon of Encouragement (15:1-7)

Azariah the son of Oded is not mentioned elsewhere. He is a prophet who meets the returning victors and preaches a sermon that (1) commends Asa's reforms for the faith, (2) reminds him that God's help has been theirs because they have been on God's side, (3) repeats the axiom that they who seek God find God and they who forsake God are abandoned by God, and (4) urges Asa on to more fervent reforms, warning against laxity. The *Spirit of God* inspires the prophetic message. According to Azariah, one cannot assume God's help if one does not cleave to God. This verse repeats the main theme of Chronicles. Having stated the theme, the sermon, typically Levitical, traces Hebrew history (see Judges 17:6-13). This historical review reminds Asa and Judah what happens when the people forsake God (see Judges 2:18-23; 3:9). The sermon is characteristic of the message of the prophetic books in the Bible.

The Covenant Celebration (15:8-15)

These verses echo the account of reforms in 14:2-5. If this is not a mere repetition of the earlier account, it suggests that the earlier reforms had not been as zealous or thorough as the ones now undertaken by the king. (The parallel passage is 1 Kings 15:9-15.) There is no previous account of the cities which he had taken from the Northern Kingdom. These were border cities over which Judah and Israel frequently fought. The *altar* was built by Solomon (8:12). There are several references in 2 Chronicles to northern Israelites who, loyal to God and the worship in Jerusalem, deserted to Judah's king. They assemble in Jerusalem *in the third month*. This may coincide with the feast of Weeks (Exodus 23:16). It also may coincide with a victory celebration.

Throughout the Chronicles are records of occasional renewals of covenant. This one, between the king and the people, is a *covenant* (verse 12) *to seek the* LORD. The frequent identification of the Lord as *the God of their fathers* (NIV; NRSV = *ancestors*) distinguishes *the God of Israel* (verse 13) from any substitute god. To *seek the* LORD is the essential description of piety for the Chronicler. Those who do not seek the Lord *should be put to death*. The Chronicler insists on the distinction of Hebrew faith (see Deuteronomy 13:6-10), which sternly keeps it from syncretization with the more permissive religions of the surrounding culture. The people affirm the covenant by taking *oath to the* LORD.

In verse 15 are four basic thematic phrases of the Chronicler's message: *All Judah rejoiced . . . with all their heart* (NRSV; NIV = *wholeheartedly*) . . . *sought him* and *he was found by them . . . the* LORD *gave them rest*. Rejoicing and rest are fundamental consequences of a people seeking God with all their hearts (or with *a whole heart*).

Asa's Zeal for the House of the Lord (15:16-19)

The firmness of Asa in fulfilling the oath is demonstrated in verses 16-18 (the parallel is 1 Kings 15:13-15). If Abijah reigned only three years (13:2), and his son, Asa, reigned forty-one years (16:13), then Asa must have been a child on coming to the throne and Maacah would have been regent. She, then, would be the person responsible for the upsurge of pagan religion that Asa sought to stamp out. *Asherah* was a goddess of fertility associated with the male fertility god, Baal. The asherah was often just a wooden pole covered with metal. It could be crushed and *burned*. *Kidron* is a ravine between the city of Jerusalem and the Mount of Olives. The *high places* seem to have remained until Hezekiah's time (31:1). Verse 18 refers to spoils of war dedicated to the Temple. There *was no more war*, that is, subsequent to the invasion by Zerah (14:9-14).

Border Struggles With Israel (16:1-6)

This passage parallels 1 Kings 15:17-22. *Baasha* is already dead by the time of Asa's twenty-sixth year, according to 1 Kings 16:8. If, however, his war with Asa takes place in the latter's sixteenth year, this would be the thirty-sixth year since Israel divided from Judah. According to 15:9, a large number of defectors from the north are among the assembly at the celebration of the covenant after Asa's victory over Zerah and the Ethiopians. This is the occasion for Baasha to build *Ramah*, a high fortification in the hills near the border between Ephraim (Israel's southern state) and Benjamin (Judah's northern state), to prevent further desertions of his people to Judah.

To meet this threat, instead of relying wholly on the Lord (14:11), Asa seeks to distract Baasha by bribing Ben-hadad, king of Syria, to invade his northern borders. To persuade Ben-hadad to break an alliance Baasha had made with him, Asa sends him *silver and gold* from the temple treasury. According to 1 Kings 15:18, he takes *all* that was left after Shishak had pillaged the Temple treasury (12:9). The Temple serves as the national treasury but, to the Chronicler, Asa is not only relying on worldly things instead of on God, he is robbing God to do so.

Ben-hadad does well for himself. Besides the treasure from Asa's kingdom, he captures valuable territory from northern Israel. *Naphtali* is a fertile district with a pleasant climate, lying west of the Sea of Galilee and reaching north almost to Mount Lebanon, where the city of *Ijon* is located. *Dan* and *Abel-maim* are cities a little to the south of Ijon. *The store-cities of Naphtali* might be storage dumps for armies in the north, but the Greek translation from an early Hebrew manuscript puts it: *from the surrounding parts of Naphtali. Geba* and *Mizpah* are hilltop lookout points east and north of Ramah. This indicates that Asa captures that area from Baasha.

Hanani's Sermon of Condemnation (16:7-10)

Azariah's sermon (15:1-7), after the battle with Zerah, commended Asa for relying on the Lord. Now Hanani's sermon, after the conflict with Baasha, condemns Asa for forsaking the Lord.

Hanani the seer is of a higher order than the ordinary seer employed by a king. He dares to rebuke the king for failure in his loyalty to Israel's God. His words are more like those of the statesmen-prophets of a later period, and this rebuke is like Isaiah's rebuke of Ahaz over a century and a quarter later (see Isaiah 7). Like Asa, Ahaz trusted a foreign alliance rather than the Lord to protect him from an enemy. Asa's sin is that he does not *rely* on the Lord, as he had when facing Zerah's invasion (14:11), but relies on the king of Syria. *The army of the king of Syria has escaped you.* That seems unimportant. Asa is not at war with Syria. Actually, however, Asa had invited Syria's attention to Israel-Judah. In taking land from the Northern Kingdom, Syria was not only invading Israel, God's people, but would continue to trouble Israel and Judah.

Hanani points out that, in contrast, by relying wholly on the Lord, Asa's army wiped out the escaping *Cushites/Ethiopians and the Libyans* (14:12-13). No Libyans are mentioned in association with Ethiopians in 14:9-13. Libyans, however, controlled Egypt at that time. Judah tended to attribute to Egypt (and so, to the controlling Libyans) any invasion from the south.

The *eyes of the LORD range throughout the earth.* This line is from Zechariah 4:10 and reflects the wider concept of God as responsive to everyone. *You have done foolishly* is what Samuel also said to Saul (1 Samuel 13:13). Saul is the Chronicler's prime example of faithlessness to God.

Asa is angry, and puts Hanani *in the stocks* (NRSV; NIV = *in prison*). The word *stocks* is used for an instrument causing pain, such as twisting the body (Jeremiah) and here, perhaps, mutilating the feet. Asa also oppressed Hanani's supporters. Such treatment was not uncommon and was considered a king's prerogative.

Asa's End (16:11-14)

These verses parallel 1 Kings 15:23-24. The Chronicler's source must have included more than what in our Bibles is simply called 1 Kings. Verse 12 implies that Asa's disease is his punishment for having failed to rely on the Lord. The disease *in his feet* is not explained, but might well be poetic justice for his cruelty to the Lord's spokesman, Hanani, and his followers. *He did not seek* the LORD, but sought help *from physicians* is a parallel to his seeking help from the king of Syria instead of relying on the Lord. His *severe* suffering lasts two years.

Burial with *spices* to preserve the body, and making a great *fire*, are customary honors for a dead king. After all, Asa's heart was *blameless all his days* (15:17 [NRSV; NIV = *committed to the* LORD *all his life*]).

§ § § § § § §

The Message of 2 Chronicles 14–16

King Asa is eager to strengthen his people's faithfulness to the God of their ancestors. This makes it possible for God to defeat the otherwise overwhelming army of invaders. When, however, Asa relies on a foreign king to help in war, and on physicians to help in sickness rather than turning to God, he is condemned for not seeking God. In this account the Chronicler is repeating his message to his readers.

It is a reminder that God sees and knows everyone's motives.

It assures all whose hearts are blameless toward God and who seek God that:

§ God is with them while they are with God.

§ They will have peace and rest.

§ God protects those who trust and obey.

§ There is great joy in uniting with others in loyalty to God and in worshiping God.

It encourages all who do right and good to:

§ Turn away from alien religion.

§ Seek God with all their heart and with all their soul.

§ Keep true to their inherited faith with its laws and its commandments.

§ Act vigorously in the disciplines of faith.

§ Fear no foe, no matter how great, as long as they rely on God.

It warns them:

§ Do not put reliance on humanity instead of on God, for even if it helps for a while, in the long run you will have continual distress.

§ If you forsake God, you separate yourself from God's help.

§ § § § § § §

2 Chronicles 17–20

Introduction to These Chapters

For the Chronicler, Jehoshaphat is one of the greater kings in the line of David. The writer chooses episodes in this king's career that show how his reign was good. The mishaps that do occur in his reign are mainly due to participating in enterprises of evil kings of northern Israel. Jehoshaphat tries to outweigh these mistakes by more vigorous actions for the education and judication of his people, and these actions are approved of by God. As with Asa, God triumphs over the king's enemies when he and the people rely on God.

Here is an outline of these chapters.
  I. Jehoshaphat's Piety and Prosperity (17:1-6)
  II. Jehoshaphat, the Religious Educator (17:7-9)
  III. Jehoshaphat's Greatness (17:10-19)
  IV. Jehoshaphat's Alliance With Ahab (18:1–19:3)
    A. A marriage and military alliance (18:1-3)
    B. Micaiah and the false prophets (18:4-27)
    C. The battle with Ramoth-gilead (18:28-34)
    D. Jehoshaphat scolded (19:1-3)
  V. Jehoshaphat's Judicial System (19:4-11)
  VI. Jehoshaphat's Victory (20:1-30)
    A. The incursion into Judah (20:1-4)
    B. Prayer and oracle of assurance (20:5-17)
    C. Praise, victory and blessing (20:18-30)
  VII. Jehoshaphat's Last Days (20:31-34)
  VIII. The Wreck of Merchant Ships (20:35-37)

Jehoshaphat's Piety and Prosperity (17:1-6)

The LORD was with Jehoshaphat, as with Solomon (1:1). To *seek* (NRSV; NIV = *consult*) *the Baals* would be to forsake the Lord, but Jehoshaphat *sought* the Lord. Baals are the earth gods worshiped to ensure reproduction (1 Kings 16:31-33; chapter 18). The Lord rewards Jehoshaphat because he follows in God's way and demolishes the worship of *Asherim* (plural of Asherah, goddess of fertility).

Jehoshaphat, the Religious Educator (17:7-9)

Jehoshaphat's concern that his people seek the Lord is shown by his program to instruct all the people in the law. The law is based on material in what is now included in the first five books of the Bible. It includes civil, criminal, and economic law, in terms of the covenant—Israel's relationship with God.

Two priests, eight Levites (the ninth name, *Tobadonijah,* is a recopying of two names), led by five *officials,* lay government leaders, are sent to interpret the law. In each town, they assemble the people to hear the law read and explained.

Jehoshaphat's Greatness (17:10-19)

Jehoshaphat's desire to strengthen his people's faithfulness to God affects neighboring nations so that they respect him and his God *and they did not make war.* Some neighbors, Philistines to the west and Arabs to the south, maintain good relations by giving gifts. Like his predecessors Solomon, Rehoboam, and Asa, Jehoshaphat's faithfulness enables him to fortify cities and build storehouses (verses 12-13; see 8:3-6; 11:5-12; 14:6). The *forces* (NRSV; NIV = *troops*) and *garrisons* of verse 2 are described (verses 12-19). *Thousands* is a general word for army units.

A Marriage and Military Alliance (18:1-3)

Royal marriages are made to strengthen diplomatic ties. This marriage arrangement is between Jehoshaphat's son, Jehoram, and Athaliah, the daughter of Israel's king, Ahab (21:5-6). *Samaria* is Israel's capital.

Ahab entertains Jehoshaphat and his retinue with a great feast. In the celebration, he persuades Jehoshaphat to join him in a military venture. The Hebrew verb *induced* (NRSV; NIV = *urged*) implies drawing away from faithfulness to God (as the word is used in Deuteronomy 13:6). *Ramoth-gilead* is a city at the edge of Israel and Syria, east of the Jordan.

Micaiah and the False Prophets (18:4-27)

Seers (called *prophets* in this passage) or soothsayers are attached to every court. No king undertakes a war or other large enterprise without consulting them. These prophets represent the current syncretism of Baal worship with the word of God in northern Israel. The typical seer calculates the risk, giving a verdict that will be favorable to the king, his employer. Jehoshaphat is anxious to be sure that the enterprise is a wise one. *Micaiah* is the one true prophet in this story. Ahab hates him, for his prophecies are never good concerning the king.

These verses paint a vivid scene of the court *sitting at the threshing floor* (a hard-packed, flat area, suitable for assemblies), *at the entrance of the gate*. Conveying a message through symbolic acts is a typical way of prophesying. Iron horns represent weapons of offense.

Micaiah is the forerunner of later prophets like Amos, Hosea, and Jeremiah, who spoke boldly against apostasy. Micaiah can go along with the crowd and say what is politically popular, or he can speak courageously according to his insights into the will of God.

The vividness of the scene continues. *The messenger* wants to avoid trouble and instructs Micaiah to agree with the four hundred. So Micaiah does, but with a polite irony that is not lost (verses 14, 15). Micaiah declares that Ahab is no shepherd. *These have no master* is an allusion to the death of Ahab. The people will return in peace, but without Ahab. *Did I not tell you?* In other words: "Micaiah speaks out of personal hostility to me, therefore he is not to be taken seriously."

Micaiah uses a third prophetic method. He paints a word picture of a council meeting in heaven. It is like the meeting envisioned in Job 1:6-12, where Satan went forth from the presence of the Lord. Here, one says, *I will go, and be a lying spirit.* (Similar statements appear in Jeremiah 23:25, 36; Zechariah 13:3; John 8:44-47.) The significance is that God wants to destroy Ahab for his sin (see Psalm 18:27).

Zedekiah is stung by Micaiah's charge. It is for him a matter of professional jealousy. He makes a dramatic defense. Since, he claims, he spoke by the Lord's Spirit, how could the same Spirit speak differently in Micaiah? It must be Micaiah that speaks by a lying spirit.

The Battle with Ramoth-gilead (18:28-34)

The kings go to attack *Ramoth-gilead*. Only one prophet, suspected of lack of patriotism, opposes the enterprise. Jehoshaphat is committed to go despite his doubts.

To destroy the enemy's leaders is the surest way to victory. To protect himself, Ahab allows Jehoshaphat to be the center of the enemy's attention. The enemy does concentrate on Jehoshaphat (verse 31). He would not escape harm, but he cries out, and God helps him. Ahab cannot escape his punishment.

Jehoshaphat Scolded (19:1-3)

Jehoshaphat returns safely but is scolded by *Jehu* whose father, Hanani, had scolded Jehoshaphat's father, Asa (16:7, but see 1 Kings 16:12). Asa sought help from an unrighteous king. Jehoshaphat gives help to a king who hates the Lord. To hate God is equivalent to forsaking God. *Wrath* is an automatic divine response to faithlessness, not an expression of emotion. What saves Jehoshaphat is that *some good* is found in him. What good? He destroyed pagan idols and sought God.

Jehoshaphat's Judicial System (19:4-11)

Another step in the centralization of Hebrew society is seen here. To the old tribal justice, Jehoshaphat adds a royally appointed judicial system. His judges are to be knowledgeable in the religious law that controls civil regulations and criminal justice in all the land. Deuteronomy is a later refinement of what is being done here in Jehoshaphat's time. To bring *them back to the* Lord, to living by the law and commandments of God, Jehoshaphat tours the nation from Beersheba in the extreme south to the hill country of Ephraim, whose border cities have been taken from northern Israel. *He appointed judges* as commanded in Deuteronomy 16:18. *Fortified cities* are walled cities that are more closely related to central government than are scattered villages. The king's counsel to his judges (verse 6) fits that of Moses in Deuteronomy 1:16-17. *Taking bribes* is a common practice. Judges give verdicts in favor of the litigant giving the largest bribe (see Deuteronomy 16:19).

The court in Jerusalem is made up of both religious leaders (Levites and priests) and lay leaders. These latter, *heads of families,* are the elders who have traditional judicial authority over their extended families. This tradition is blended into Jehoshaphat's centralized court. It deals with religious law under the high priest, *Amariah,* and it deals with the king's royal law under his representative, *Zebadiah.*

In dispensing judgment, they are to decide cases that arise within Jerusalem. The king's charge (verse 9) follows Deuteronomy 17:8-13. *Deal courageously* (NRSV; NIV = *Act with courage*) means to not compromise the law (15:7; 1 Chronicles 28:20). *Officers* serve under judges in administering justice.

The Incursion into Judah (20:1-4)

The *Moabites and Ammonites* are east of the Dead Sea and the Jordan. They are joined by some *Meunites*. Meunites are an Arab tribe identified with Ma'an, a town about twelve miles southeast of Sela, a walled city of Edom. The invaders march on an unfrequented road along the west coast of the Dead Sea. At En-gedi, midway along the coast, they take a road northwestward through the Wilderness of Judah toward Bethlehem in the hills. Their approach, secret and unexpected, frightens Jehoshaphat.

Prayer and Oracle of Assurance (20:5-17)

Jehoshaphat's prayer, like Solomon's at the dedication of the Temple (chapter 6), magnifies the Lord, asks for God's help in times of disaster, recalls Israel's deliverance from Egypt as God's people, and cries for help against the invading army. The prayer is familiar in the psalms. It reminds the readers that they are distinct from other people. The land is theirs because God gave it to them. That raises a question. God would not let invading Israel destroy *Ammon and Moab and Mount Seir* (Edom) (Deuteronomy 2:4-5, 9, 19). Now these nations want to drive them out. The people do not know what to do.

Praise, Victory, and Blessing (20:18-30)

The people respond to the oracle with humility, praise, and courage. The worship is led by *the Korahites*, a guild of Levite singers. They sing *with a very loud voice* (see Psalm 42:4).

Verse 20 conveys the confidence with which the army of Judah sets out. *The wilderness* (NRSV; NIV = *desert*) *of Tekoa* is east of Tekoa, fourteen miles south of Jerusalem. Jehoshaphat encourages his troops to *believe* in God and be confident in the oracles of promise given by the *prophets*. Those who were *to sing* are the Levite Temple singers. In verse 21 *for he is good* is omitted in this quotation (see Psalm 106:1; 1 Chronicles 16:34), but it is understood. God set an ambush. The enemy soldiers turn on themselves and are soon slaughtering one another. There is a hint of tension caused by a group of the Meunites, Arab tribesmen from east of Edom.

Sentinels from the Wilderness of Judah, between the hills and the Dead Sea, have brought warning to Jehoshaphat (verse 2). The spoils are excessive for a raiding party. The Chronicler's point is that the greater the spoils, the greater the wonder that God has performed for the people who trusted.

The Valley of Beracah (Valley of Blessing) is near Tekoa. What began with prayer at the Temple (verses 5-12) now becomes praise in the Valley of Blessing and a procession of praise back to the Temple.

Jehoshaphat's Last Days (20:31-34)

This passage parallels 1 Kings 22:41-45. He *did not turn aside* (NRSV; NIV = *stray*) . . . *he did what was right.* Although he does fall into faithlessness temporarily, he cries out to God for help (18:31). *The high places* seems to contradict 17:6. If both these passages are by the same writer, the only explanation can be that, while he opposed the pagan high places of worship, and ordered them leveled, the people still held on to them.

The Wreck of Merchant Ships (20:35-37)

This fragment, inserted as a postscript, parallels 1 Kings 22:48-49. Jehoshaphat seems to have a penchant for allying himself with kings of Israel who do *wickedly.* The Chronicler interprets this as dependence on others rather than on God. That explains the disastrous outcome and calls for a rebuke by the prophet of God, Eliezer, mentioned only here (compare 19:1-3). *Ships to go to Tarshish* (see NIV footnote) must mean large sailing ships like those of Tarshish. Tarshish is on the Mediterranean Sea. Jehoshaphat's ships are at *Ezion-geber* on the Gulf of Aqaba, an arm of the Red Sea.

§ § § § § § §

The Message of 2 Chronicles 17–20

Jehoshaphat tries to get all the people of Judah to be faithful to God and to understand and keep the law. But whenever he is in a military or commercial venture, he relies on an unfaithful king (of northern Israel) instead of on God, and he fails. Whenever he calls on God, he is helped. Through this story, the Chronicler counsels his readers as follows:

§ Those who walk courageously in God's way, and do what is right in the sight of the Lord, are blessed so that their faithfulness is a witness to all.

§ Those who keep company with, and go along with, persons who are not loyal to God, instead of with God, will face disastrous consequences.

§ God's people must be instructed in and understand the law of God. Therefore:

§ Avoid the counsel of those who say what they think you want to hear, promising success no matter what you do. Follow the counsel of those whose faithfulness to God and God's word is sure.

§ Do not say what you think will be pleasing, or whatever the majority is saying. Say, with the courage of your convictions, what God would have you say.

§ Join with people who seek God, confident that God will help. You are powerless, but God can help you face every problem and crisis without fear.

§ Worship, praise, sing thanksgiving to God, and join in celebrating God's greatness and goodness.

§ Act boldly against wrong, against anything that draws people away from God.

§ Believe firmly in God and in those who speak for God, and you will be steady and not fail.

§ § § § § § §

2 Chronicles 21–24

Introduction to These Chapters

These chapters cover the reigns of Jehoram, Ahaziah, and Joash. Athaliah, as queen mother and ruler during the early childhood of Joash, represents apostasy and evil. Jehoiada as priest, son-in-law to King Ahaziah, and protector of Joash, represents faithfulness and good. All their activities demonstrate the Chronicler's teaching that faithlessness to God ends in suffering and loss of freedom; faithfulness restores peace and prosperity.

After the good reign of Jehoshaphat, Jehoram's and Ahaziah's are negative; only Joash's is positive. The Chronicler shows, through these three reigns, that God's promise of the everlasting establishment of David's line is conditioned on faithfulness to God on the part of David's descendants. Under Athaliah, David's line is almost wiped out. Joash alone redeems it, restores the worship of God, and becomes a type of David, who restored Israel after the failure of Saul. Nevertheless, Joash, like Asa and Jehoshaphat, both good kings, comes to grief when he fails in faithfulness to God.

Here is an outline of these chapters.
  I. Jehoram's Reign (21:1-20)
     A. Jehoram's evil (21:1-7)
     B. Results of Jehoram's evil (21:8-20)
 II. Ahaziah's Reign (22:1-9)
III. Athaliah Reigns; Jehoiada Revolts (22:10–23:21)
     A. Prince Joash hidden from Athaliah (22:10-12)
     B. Conspiracy and covenant (23:1-21)

IV. The Reign of Joash (24:1-27)
  A. Early years of Joash (24:1-3)
  B. Funds to repair the Temple (24:4-14)
  C. Forsaking the house of the Lord (24:15-22)
  D. The results of faithlessness (24:23-27)

Jehoram's Reign (21:1-20)

The story of Jehoram (its parallel is in 2 Kings 8:16-24) shows the dynasty of David at a low point in its history. It illustrates the Chronicler's theme that faithlessness to God brings about personal and national disaster. It shows how Jehoram's behavior violates the King David ideal. His, and Azariah's reign after him, all but destroy the hope, based on God's promise to David, that Israel and the line of David can endure.

Jehoram's Evil (21:1-7)

Reference to a king's provision for his sons is not unusual (see 11:23). Jehoshaphat's generosity to his sons stands in contrast with the slaughter of the descendants of David (21:4; 22:10). *Azariah* is repeated by mistake.

With the many gifts go administrative responsibilities. *Fortified cities* are cities strategically located for defense. *Because he was the firstborn*: Kings picked for their successors those that they thought were best qualified among their sons (as David selected Solomon). In the absence of such a decision, the throne goes to the firstborn, which seems to be Jehoram's only qualification.

Was established means that he is in control of the nation's armed forces and treasury. *He all his brothers to the sword:* This was not an infrequent occurrence when a prince wished to secure his throne against their possible ambitions. *Princes* (NIV; NRSV = *officials*) *of Israel* means princes of Judah. Because Judah represents his ideal of the true Israel, the Chronicler often calls Judah, Israel. In verse 6, however, *Israel* refers to the Northern Kingdom.

Jehoram's action marks his evil character (as in verse 13). This nearly wipes out the descendants of David (verse 7).

Results of Jehoram's Evil (21:8-20)

Jehoram attempts to quell the revolt with a surprise attack by night, but is surrounded by Edomite troops. He manages to break out, but is deserted by his own army (2 Kings 8:21). Edom, south of the Dead Sea, was conquered by David, provided wealth to Solomon because of its mines and trade, and was ruled by an appointee of the king in Jerusalem (1 Kings 22:47). Its successful revolt and the desertion of Jehoram's army, followed by the revolt of *Libnah* on the border of Philistia on the west, show how weak and despised Jehoram is. This all happens, explains the Chronicler, *because he had forsaken the LORD.*

High places are for the worship of Baal. That Jehoram's son's name, Azariah, includes the Hebrew name for God, suggests that Jehoram worshiped Baal, the Canaanite fertility god, under the name of the Hebrew God, Yahweh. *Elijah the prophet* was active in northern Israel more than a generation earlier in the time of Ahab. The Chronicler has a very old Elijah concerning himself with the affairs of Judah for the only time in his life (see 2 Kings 1:17).

Verse 13 implies that Jehoram kills his brothers because they are faithful to the Lord. In Chronicles, warnings of punishment for a king's wrongdoing are often brought by prophets. The story of Elijah's warning, of the sack of Judah, and of the disease of Jehoram, are not found in the 2 Kings accounts.

The LORD aroused: Enemies who attack Judah (or Israel) are always seen by the Chronicler to be the unwitting agents of God's judgment. *Philistines,* on the seacoast borders west of Judah, and *Arabs* frequently made fast raids. Bedouin tribes to the south of Judah were often lumped together as *Ethiopians. His sons* indicates another depletion of the descendants of David (as in verse 4). Jehoram's complete weakness, even against border raids, is due to his *unfaithfulness* to God. *Jehoahaz* is another form of the name *Ahaziah*.

The details of Jehoram's disease, prophesied by Elijah (verse 15), are graphic, but the disease can only be guessed at. The people detest Jehoram, as the Chronicler clearly records. They do not give him the usual honors for a dead king (16:14), nor do they even bury him in the royal tomb. *He died to no one's regret.*

Ahaziah's Reign (22:1-9)

There is a thread of continuity in this text that begins with 18:1. Jehoshaphat marries his son, Jehoram, to Ahab's daughter, Athaliah. Ahab has a bad influence on Jehoshaphat (21:6). After Jehoram's death, that influence continues, for Athaliah is the mother of King Ahaziah. The close alliance with Ahab's house continues. This passage also continues the threat to the line of David, despite God's promise (21:7).

Jehoram has killed all his brothers (21:4). All his sons, with the exception of Ahaziah, are captured and killed (21:17; 22:1). Even his nephews are all killed by Israel's rebel king, Jehu. After Azariah's death, his mother kills all but one of the rest of the family.

The inhabitants (NRSV; NIV = *people*) *of Jerusalem* are usually all the people who agree to the king's coronation (see 26:1). Verse 2 refers to the raiding party of 21:16-17. *Forty-two* (NRSV; NIV = *twenty-two*) may be a copyist's error, making him older than his father (21:20). Some manuscripts have *twenty*. Omri is the father of Ahab. Athaliah, like everyone else in the house of Jacob, is a forceful person, counseling her son in doing wickedly. Her family, the royal house of northern Israel, is the major influence on Ahaziah. *Ramoth-gilead* is an outpost claimed by Israel and Syria. *Jezreel* is an Israelite royal city.

This passage about Ahaziah's death assumes knowledge of the information found in 2 Kings 9:1-28 and 10:12-14. The Chronicler shows, as he did in the story of Jehoram, (1) the error of consorting with the evil rulers of northern Israel, (2) the judgment of God, and (3) the ignominy of the king's end: fleeing, hiding, being captured and killed, and buried without honors and away from the tombs of the kings. The Chronicler also emphasizes the near extinction of the descendants of David so that there is left no one able to rule the kingdom. Typically, Ahaziah's decision is planned by God so that he will be killed (note the similar way in which Ahab is brought to his death, 18:19, 21; and see 10:15). *Jehoram* is the same person as *Joram*, king of Israel. *Jehu* usurps the throne of Israel at this time.

Athaliah Reigns; Jehoiada Revolts (22:10–23:21)

This story parallels 2 Kings 11:1-21. *Athaliah* is the daughter (some sources suggest sister) of Israel's King Ahab, queen wife of Judah's King Jehoram, queen mother of Judah's King Ahaziah, and ruler of Judah for a short time after her son's death. *Jehoiada* is the high priest at the Temple in Jerusalem.

This passage has four emphases: (1) the evil influence of the house of Ahab in Judah, expressed through Queen Athaliah; (2) the struggle to return to faithfulness to God through Jehoiada; (3) the joyful support by all the people of that return; and (4) God's intervention to save the almost extinct line of David on Judah's throne (see 2 Kings 11:1-3).

Prince Joash Hidden from Athaliah (22:10-12)

The Chronicler does not consider that Athaliah, of the house of Ahab, is truly queen of Judah. She seizes the throne and tries to extinguish the heirs of David (verse 10). From now on, as the Chronicler reviews history, *Joash*, the only surviving heir to David, is the true king.

Princess *Jehoshabeath* saves the throne for God's promised heir of David by hiding Joash in the Temple.

Conspiracy and Covenant (23:1-21)

Jehoiada is the heroic figure of this period. He has the courage to conspire against Queen Athaliah, who spared no one standing in her way. He draws the people to his causes: the restoration of the line of David, a return to faithful worship, respect for the holy Temple, and the reinstitution of the *priests* and *Levites* in the orders of their service.

Jehoiada's religious authority gives him opportunity to move about the country among the Levites, the religious professionals. The unpopularity of the queen makes them and the elders of each town, *the heads of families*, quick to enter his service.

They assemble in the courts of the house of the Lord (the Temple). Levite guards are placed in appropriate places and, before the queen is aware of what is happening, they make a covenant with the young King Joash, who is brought out of hiding, and agree to Jehoiada's suggestion to let him reign. Levite guards surround him to protect him.

The gathering of people at the Temple on the sabbath is normal, except that the crowd is larger. It is normal for Levites to come on duty on the sabbath to replace the *divisions* who are on duty from the previous sabbath, except that, in this case, the replaced Levites do not leave but remain to double the guard. The ritual of coronation proceeds, ending with a shout: *Long live the king*.

What Queen Athaliah sees and hears and her cry of horror are vividly described. The acclamation by *all the people* is a reminder of the people acclaiming David as king to replace Saul (1 Chronicles 11:1-3). They want to *bring her out between the ranks*, that is, from the Temple precincts. Blood spilled in the Temple would pollute it.

The Chronicler stresses Jehoiada's leadership in restoring the ideal righteous kingdom. This kingdom includes the ministry of the Levitical priests and the Levites as organized by David (see 1 Chronicles 15, 16), and the Temple worship as *written in the law of Moses* (verse 18). All the people rededicate the nation in a solemn *covenant* with the high priest and the king. The celebration is led by singing Levites *according to the order of David* (see 1 Chronicles 23:4-5 [NRSV; NIV = *as David had ordered*]). *Baal* is the pagan fertility god worshiped by the royal family of Israel.

The Reign of Joash (24:1-27)

In the Chronicler's account (parallel to 2 Kings 12), the reign of Joash is successful because *Jehoiada instructed him* (2 Kings 12:2). Joash even takes major responsibility to restore the Temple.

When Jehoiada dies, however, Joash comes under the influence of *officials of Judah*, who push him to support pagan fertility worship. Thus, the Chronicler contrasts the king's zeal for the Temple with his later neglect of it, even killing the prophet who warns him. The Chronicler explains the scourge of an invading Syrian army and the assassination of Joash as a judgment for the king's weakness.

Early Years of Joash (24:1-3)

Jehoiada is, in effect, the regent or the protector of the king. The king does what is right as long as Jehoiada is alive. Jehoiada even procures his wives. He has children. Having children is not only a sign of the Lord's blessing (as in 11:18-23; 13:21) but is also a reassurance that the almost extinguished dynasty of David will be restored.

Funds to Repair the Temple (24:4-14)

Verse 7 explains why the Temple is in disrepair. Joash pushes for speedy restoration. Here, as in most episodes in the Chronicles, *the priests and Levites* are the main actors. *All Israel* is the Chronicler's word for the people of Judah who ideally represent David's Israel.

The reluctance of the *Levites* to carry out the king's orders is not explained. They may feel that the king's order is an infringement on their rights. By Mosaic law, they are supported by the tithes brought to them by the people (Numbers 18:21-24).

The king is expected to keep the Temple in repair from his own resources. Joash tries to change that. They resent the extra duty of going out to collect the *tax levied by Moses* (Exodus 30:11-16). The Chronicler maintains the continuity of the Temple with *the tent of testimony* (NIV; NRSV = *tent of the covenant*) at which Israel worshiped in the desert journey. The king has an alternative plan for raising money. *Outside the gate*, the lay people, forbidden to enter the Temple itself, can give their money. The Chronicler notes the people's joy in Temple activities (as in 1 Chronicles 29:9). Continual offering of *burnt offerings* is evidence of faithfulness to God.

Forsaking the House of the Lord (24:15-22)

The champion of loyalty to the Lord dies. *Old and full of days*: This phrase is reserved for persons who have lived well and honorably (as in Genesis 25:8; Job 42:17). Long life is a blessing from God for those who have lived a faithful life. Unworthy kings, like Jehoram (21:20) and Ahaziah (22:9), are not buried among the kings. Jehoiada, not a king, is worthy to be among them as agent of God's rule.

Apparently, many of the people and their *officials* have continued to worship and trust in the old fertility gods (as noted in 2 Kings 12:3). *Asherim* are female fertility gods. When people forsake God and *the house* (or *temple*) *of the* LORD (the worship of God), they always, in Chronicles, trip the divine judgment: The wrath of God comes upon them (as in 19:2). Also, when they forsake God they arouse prophets who exhort them to return to God, although usually in vain (as in 2 Kings 17:13-14; Jeremiah 7:25-26). Sometimes the king repents and God forgives (12:5-7), and sometimes the king is infuriated with the prophet (as in 16:9-10). In this case, Joash angrily commands the death of the preacher, Zechariah, even though, says the Chronicler, he is the son of Jehoiada, by whose aid Joash had his throne. The warning: *You have forsaken the LORD,* he has forsaken you is the basic theme in 2 Chronicles 12:5; 15:2. The opposite, too, is in effect: Put faith in God and you will prosper (20:20; 26:5). The warning often begins in the form of a question like Zechariah's: *Why do you transgress,* since, of course, you must know the result: *You cannot prosper.*

They stone him in the courtyard. The holy place of their violent act makes it that much worse (see Luke 11:51). Zechariah's dying call for vengeance is answered in verse 25.

The Results of Faithlessness (24:23-27)

According to 2 Kings 12:17-18, Joash buys off Hazael, king of Syria. The Chronicler, however, records the devastation inflicted by the army of the Syrians to point out the punishment meted out to Judah for its apostasy. In contrast to the overwhelming armies overcome by Judah's reliance on the Lord (as in 14:9-15; 20:12, 17), here an army with just a few men overcomes Judah's large army, because the people of Judah had forsaken the LORD. Judah's victories have really been the Lord's. Here, the defeat is brought about by the Lord, who delivers them into the hands of the Syrians, who in turn execute God's judgment on Joash.

Joash is assassinated (2 Kings 12:20). The Chronicler says he was severely wounded in battle for having *forsaken the LORD* (verse 20). He is killed by his servants for killing Zechariah, son of the good priest, Jehoiada. *They conspired against him*: This is poetic justice, using the same phrase as in verse 21 at the stoning of Zechariah. The Chronicler notes that the two men who kill Joash are sons of foreign women. There is further judgment in that the people do not honor him as Jehoiada was honored by burial in the royal tombs.

§ § § § § § §

The Message of 2 Chronicles 21–24

These stories of four sovereigns of Judah differ in their situations and relationships according to the circumstances of the times. They are judged, however, by unchanging, universal realities, which are, according to Chronicles:

§ Forsake God and God forsakes you.

§ Nevertheless, God will warn you when you go wrong.

§ If you heed the warning and turn back to God, God forgives and helps you.

§ If you refuse the warning, you face disaster.

§ If you harm God's messenger, God will punish you.

§ If you rely on God, God will defeat overwhelming odds against you and save you.

§ If you rely on persons or forces not of God, they will fail you.

§ If you trust God and those who speak for God, you will succeed.

These principles are illustrated by character types:

§ The purely selfish, like Jehoram, are despised by the people.

§ Others, like Ahaziah, desire only pleasure with their own kind and ignore God, the law, and the people. They end up isolated and defeated.

§ Some, like Athaliah, who assert their will at any cost to others, end up resented by all.

§ People like Jehoiada, with courage and wisdom to lead society against evil, end up full of honors.

§ Unstable persons, like Joash, under good guidance support good works, but under evil influence neglect faith and lose their way.

§ § § § § § §

1 AND 2 CHRONICLES

2 Chronicles 25–28

Introduction to These Chapters

These chapters interpret the reigns of the tenth through thirteenth kings in David's dynasty, kings of Judah: Amaziah, Uzziah, Jotham, and Ahaz. Like all the preceding reigns, these are judged in light of God's overrule. Ideally, all Israel is God's people, God's kingdom is based in Jerusalem, and all the kings of Judah are inheritors of the promise to David. Thus these kings are blessed when they are faithful to God, punished when they are unfaithful, condemned when they fail to rely on God, but forgiven when they repent. The Chronicler is careful to note that every success or failure in each reign is caused by the king's goodness or badness. He gives Amaziah and Uzziah a mixed score, Jotham a casually favorable evaluation, and Ahaz a negative one.

Here is an outline of these chapters.
  I. The Reign of Amaziah (25:1-28)
     A. Amaziah's qualified rightness (25:1-4)
     B. Amaziah's military activities (25:5-13)
     C. Amaziah worships Edomite gods (25:14-16)
     D. Amaziah's conflict with Israel (25:17-24)
     E. Amaziah's end (25:25-28)
  II. The Reign of Uzziah (26:1-23)
     A. Uzziah's good beginning (26:1-5)
     B. Uzziah's strength in foreign affairs (26:6-8)
     C. Uzziah's strength in domestic affairs (26:9-15)

  D. Uzziah's pride and his leprosy (26:16-21)
  E. Uzziah's end (26:22-23)
 III. The Reign of Jotham (27:1-9)
 IV. The Reign of Ahaz (28:1-27)
  A. The evil religious practices of Ahaz (28:1-4)
  B. Judah's defeat by Syria and Israel (28:5-7)
  C. Return of the captives to Judah (28:8-15)
  D. Judah's affliction by Assyria (28:16-21)
  E. Increasing apostasy and end of Ahaz (28:22-27)

Amaziah's Qualified Rightness (25:1-4)

Reasons for the Chronicler's *yet not with a* (NRSV; NIV = *not wholeheartedly*) *true heart* may be found in 25:14-16 and in 2 Kings 14:3-4. Amaziah executes those responsible for killing his father (see 24:25-26), but does not kill *their children,* a moral advance over past and contemporary practice (see 2 Kings 9:26). The law is explained in Deuteronomy 24:16.

Amaziah's Military Activities (25:5-13)

This passage parallels 2 Kings 14:7. It is expected of new kings that they prove themselves in a war. The nation of Edom, until its successful revolt under King Jehoram (21:8-10), was subject to Judah. Amaziah will fight them. First, however, he will study his military potential, then muster an army from his two provinces, *Judah and Benjamin.* Thinking that the army is not strong enough, he hires mercenaries from Israel. An unnamed prophet, *a man of God,* appears to warn the king against using the *Ephraimites.* Ephraim, the province just north of Judah, is often used as a title for northern Israel. The reasons given by the prophet are that (1) Israel as a nation has forsaken God (13:4-12), and (2) using them means relying on a human force instead of on God. Historically there could have been a third reason: northern Israel's friendship for Edom, which would make the mercenaries actually unreliable.

Amaziah accepts the prophet's advice. One hundred talents is an enormous sum, equal to about three and a half tons of silver. The prophet's faith is that the LORD is able *to give you much more*. The discharged mercenaries are, not surprisingly, very angry. Besides payment for actual service, they have, according to custom, a right to a share in the spoils of victory. They take it out on the border towns of Judah (in Benjamin) on their way home (verse 13). Because *Samaria* is far north into Israel, this may be a miscopy of the name *Migron*, which, at a quick glance, looks similar to *Samaria* in Hebrew script. From Migron *to Beth-horon* would be a swath of towns along the border of the two countries.

With the courage of the prophet's assurance, Amaziah has a great victory. The army of Edom must meet the army of Judah at *the Valley of Salt* at the southern extreme of Judah and west of the Dead Sea. Their homeland is in the mountain range of *Seir*, southeast of the Dead Sea.

Amaziah Worships Edomite Gods (25:14-16)

Normally a victorious army raids the enemy's Temple treasury and takes away the images of their gods. In this way, they seize the enemy's source of power (see 1 Samuel 5:1-2). Amaziah does this. Prophetic condemnation often, in Chronicles, takes the form of a question. The gods are obviously powerless before the Lord. If the king had *humbled himself* (as in 12:12), *the wrath of the LORD* would have turned from him. Instead, King Amaziah retorts insolently. The prophet withdraws with a threat. God's warning has turned into a determination to destroy him.

Amaziah's Conflict with Israel (25:17-24)

Having rejected the counsel of the Lord's prophet (verse 16), the king is wholly dependent on human counsel now. Lifted up in confidence because of his victory over Edom, forgetting the source of that victory, Amaziah invites Israel's king to battle. Israel's King Joash sends a picturesquely taunting reply: *Why should you provoke trouble?*

Amaziah's doom is inevitable. He has rebuffed the Lord's spokesman, repudiated his warning. He relies no longer on God, but on human resources and even on playthings, like the Edomite idols. In fact, God has already determined Amaziah's punishment. So actually it is to God that Amaziah will not listen (see 22:7).

Because *Beth-shemesh* is far to the west and a little south of Jerusalem, the army of northern Israel must flank Judah before Amaziah's army is ready. The defeat is a rout, even the king being captured. Joash breaks down probably about 600 feet of the wall built by Solomon, extending from a gate in the north wall to the northwest corner. *Obed-edom* is, according to 1 Chronicles 26:16, the family in charge of the Temple storehouse.

Amaziah's End (25:25-28)

This passage is close to 2 Kings 14:17-20. The Chronicler adds that Amaziah fails as a king from the time he starts worshiping the Edomite gods. The conspiracy suggests his growing unpopularity. *Lachish* is a well-fortified city southwest of Jerusalem.

Uzziah's Good Beginning (26:1-5)

These lines parallel 2 Kings 14:21-22; 15:2-3. According to the Chronicler, Amaziah does not leave a high standard to his son, Uzziah, for doing what is right. Nevertheless, he does seek God while he is under the guidance of *Zechariah*. As a result *God gave him success* (NIV; NRSV = *made him prosper*).

Eloth, seaport at the head of the Gulf of Aqaba, was lost to the Edomites during the reign of Jehoram. Uzziah establishes himself among kings by recapturing it.

Uzziah's Strength in Foreign Affairs (26:6-8)

The key phrases here are: *God helped him . . . his fame spread . . . he became very powerful* (NIV; NRSV = *strong*).

Gath, Jabneh, and *Ashdod* are major cities in Philistia east of Judah. Uzziah builds these cities as settlements of Judah that will help control the territory and prevent further raids. Bedouin tribes often swoop up from the south to coincide with the perennial raids of *the Philistines.* These Arabs are from *Gurbaal,* east of Judah's southern outpost, Beersheba. *The Meunites* may come from farther southeast in desert country (see the comments on 20:1). *The Ammonites* live east of the lower Jordan. This list indicates the vastness of Uzziah's power.

Uzziah's Strength in Domestic Affairs (26:9-15)

These verses show Uzziah as a busy, able administrator of many interests. Building activities are a characteristic of God's blessing.

Uzziah strengthens Jerusalem and builds towers for the defense of his flocks. *The Shephelah* (NRSV; NIV = *foothills*) are the fertile foothills west of Jerusalem. *In the plain* means east of the Dead Sea.

Besides a standing army, Uzziah's officers develop a people's army of conscript reserves. He also develops an ongoing armament industry to have an army ready-equipped for war. His soldiers will not be responsible, as in former times, for bringing with them whatever armament they have. *He made machines:* something like catapults, which are not known to have been invented in Uzziah's day.

The key to this section is the last verse, like verse 8, which is a summary of Uzziah's accomplishments.

Uzziah's Pride and His Leprosy (26:16-21)

Uzziah becomes proud, and pride is the opposite of reliance on God.

An affliction, such as leprosy, is believed to be divine punishment for sin, and therefore the sinner is forbidden to enter the Temple precincts. According to Leviticus 13, priests determine if a person has leprosy, and if he does, he is considered unclean and must live separately from others. One symptom is described as a burn on the skin (Leviticus 13:24-28). The suggestion is that the burn of leprosy comes upon Uzziah from the *censer*. Azariah, the priest, warns the king that the function of burning incense in the Temple is reserved to the priest alone (see 26:6). *You have done wrong*, he says. If he had repented humbly, he would have been forgiven, but Uzziah is angry, and for that he is punished. For a similar situation see 16:9-10; 1 Kings 13:1-4. Unclean, having to live apart, Uzziah can no longer effectively rule and gives that responsibility to his son, Jotham.

Uzziah's End (26:22-23)

Isaiah begins his ministry at the end of Uzziah's career (Isaiah 1:1; 6:1). Uzziah is buried alone.

The Reign of Jotham (27:1-9)

This section parallels 2 Kings 15:32-38. Jotham reigns sixteen years, about eleven of them as regent for his father. The Chronicler has nothing to say against Jotham, and little praise. The *corrupt practices* of the people are described in 2 Kings 15:35. He continues his father's work of improving the defenses of Jerusalem. *The wall* (NRSV; NIV = hill) *of Ophel* is a spur in the southern wall of the Temple grounds. He maintains his father's overlordship of the *Ammonites*, east of the lower Jordan (verse 5). Because the Ammonites are so distant from Judah, some scholars think that Meunites, the people of Maon (Ma'an), are meant here (as in 26:7-8). The secret of Jotham's might is stated in verse 6. *All his wars* may refer to the attacks mentioned in 2 Kings 15:37.

The Evil Religious Practices of Ahaz (28:1-4)

Any worship but that of the Lord of righteousness is condemned (see 13:8-9; Isaiah 2:6-8, 20-21). Ahaz worships ancient fertility gods, such as the *Baals*, lords of the soil. They are worshiped on *high places*, tree-crowned hills, or raised platforms with altars. Especially notorious is *the valley of the son of Hinnom*, a deep ravine south of Jerusalem where cultic ceremonies include the sacrifice of children to assure fertility.

Judah's Defeat by Syria and Israel (28:5-7)

The disasters recorded here (see Isaiah 7:2, 4) are because the people have forsaken God. God, who is in charge of history, gives Judah *into the hand of* (NRSV; NIV = *over to*) *the king of Aram* and *into the hand of the king of Israel . . . Pekah*. These kings are merely agents of God's judgment. The Chronicler spells out the enormity of Judah's defeat, in which not only many thousands of *men of valor* but also even persons close to the king are killed. *Ephraim* is the major province of Israel.

Return of the Captives to Judah (28:8-15)

This story of mercy reminded the Chronicler's readers of the greater captivity and later return of the exiles of Judah in the sixth century. The God who punishes Judah for apostasy also restores them because of the enduring promise. In this case, the agents of God's judgment against Judah, who are themselves a part of Israel, and apostate, repent and become God's agents of mercy.

A prophet warns the northern Israel army. But (northern) Israel has sins of its own (verses 10, 13). It is the Lord's action that enables Israel to capture Judah. This same Lord's fierce wrath is upon Israel for their *sins and guilt*. Not the king of Israel, but some of the leaders of *Ephraim*, the province into which the army had brought its captives, repent, heed the prophet's warning, stop the army, and demand the return of the captives. This action, together with the compassionate treatment of the captives, runs counter to prevailing custom, which gives conquering armies the right to exterminate or enslave their enemies and take the spoils for themselves.

Above all, the Chronicler underlines the kinship of one people with one Lord God.

Jericho, north of the Dead Sea, was a convenient place in Judah to leave the refugees for their own return home.

Judah's Affliction by Assyria (28:16-21)

Uzziah, grandfather of Ahaz, took part of Philistia and built cities there (26:6). Edom was long a satellite of Judah. Now Judah is so weak that Philistia and Edom reverse the process. *The Shephelah* (NRSV; NIV = *foothills*) are the foothills between the hills of Judah and Philistia in the west. The cities mentioned are important fortified cities of Judah in that region. The *Negeb* is south of Judah. The reason for Judah's weakness is Ahaz. The Chronicler says that he is *faithless*, that is, to the Temple, to the purity of its worship, and in serving foreign gods.

The Chronicler frequently speaks of *help* that comes from God to those who ask for it. Totally separated from God, a helpless Ahaz applies to the growing power of Assyria for help. But, because Ahaz robs the Temple to pay tribute to Assyria, no help comes. Instead, *Tilgath-pilneser king of Assyria* afflicts him.

Increasing Apostasy and End of Ahaz (28:22-27)

Ahaz grows religiously frantic. His total turn away from God leads him to pillage and close the Temple, the unifying source of Judah's and Israel's relationship with God. Rashly he tries for help from *the gods of Damascus*. But they prove to be no help at all.

As with other apostate kings, Ahaz is not worthy of being buried in *the tombs of the kings of Israel*.

§ § § § § § §

The Message of 2 Chronicles 25–28

Four kings of Judah in succession start their reigns with the opportunities and possibilities that come with responsibility. According to the Chronicler, Amaziah, Uzziah, and Jotham obey God, but personal pride brings reverses to Amaziah and suffering to Uzziah. Ahaz, on the other hand, ignores God, depends on the ways of the world, and brings his nation to disaster.

The Chronicler wrote these accounts to help his readers understand why a great people of God could, by abandoning God, become separated from God and from their land. This account is also a reminder that, whatever they do, they can inherit God's promise and plan for them through repentance and return.

The message, applicable to all readers, is:

§ Life is a responsibility to do what is right in the eyes of the Lord.

§ People unfaithful to God are not to be relied on.

§ Pride is non-reliance on God and leads to self-destruction.

§ The *abominable practices of the nations* are to be strictly avoided.

§ To worship, support, or follow substitutes for the God in whom our ancestors believed brings disaster.

§ The counsel of God's messengers is to be heeded.

§ Trust in God brings success to all undertakings.

§ Persons should not take advantage of wrongdoers, but should remember their own sin and guilt.

§ Enemies in distress should be treated with compassion since they also are in God's care.

§ No one should be punished for the guilt of another.

§ § § § § § §

2 Chronicles 29–32

Introduction to These Chapters

These chapters are the Chronicler's message of
assurance and hope to his readers. In the story of Ahaz
(chapter 28), the Chronicler showed what happened to a
nation whose people and leaders were unfaithful to God:
collapse and captivity. His readers were living in the
aftermath of such a collapse. These chapters show what
happens to a nation whose people and leader return to
faithfulness in worship. This gives hope to his readers
that restoration can happen again.

These chapters may be outlined as follows.
  I. Restoration of Temple Worship (29:1-36)
     A. Hezekiah's good reign (29:1-2)
     B. The cleansing of the Temple (29:3-19)
     C. Reinstitution of Temple worship (29:20-36)
 II. The Renewal of Israel (30:1-27)
     A. Invitation to all Israel to return (30:1-12)
     B. The unity of God's people (30:13-27)
III. Renewal of Right Religious Practices (31:1-21)
     A. Destruction of pagan religion (31:1)
     B. Contributions to the Temple service (31:2-10)
     C. Organization of the priests and Levites (31:11-19)
     D. Hezekiah's service to the house of God (31:20-21)
 IV. The Threat from Assyria (32:1-23)
  V. The Close of Hezekiah's Reign (32:24-33)

Hezekiah's Good Reign (29:1-2)

The brief introduction prepares for an expanded description of how Hezekiah *did what was right*.

The Cleansing of the Temple (29:3-19)

In the first year . . . first month leaves no doubt of the king's urgent priority. He opens the doors that Ahaz had closed (see 28:24). He brings in the priests and Levites, for they only, by Mosaic law, can enter the Temple, and then only after they cleanse themselves (1 Chronicles 15:12). Verse 6 sums up the essence of evil for the Chronicler, echoing the warning given to Solomon in 7:21-22.

Hezekiah's address to the Levites (verses 9-11) carries a special message to the Chronicler's contemporaries. Their fathers were taken in captivity at the great Exile (597 and 586 B.C.), and they dare not neglect the worship of God in what is now the Second Temple, Solomon's having been destroyed.

The Levites respond promptly. The names represent four (two names apiece) great Levite families, and three (two names apiece) families of Levite musicians (1 Chronicles 15–16). The priests clean out the *inner part*, which only priests are allowed to enter. *The brook Kidron*, between Jerusalem and the Mount of Olives east of the city, is the city's rubbish dump. They consecrate each part as they clean it. The *utensils* (NRSV; NIV = *articles*) are used in worship at the altar of burnt offering in front of the Temple. The table for the showbread, where fresh loaves are placed each week, is inside the Temple.

Reinstitution of Temple Worship (29:20-36)

The seven bulls, rams, and lambs are used as a petition for reconciliation with God. The seven he-goats are for a sin offering in atonement for the sins of the king, priests, and all the people. The significance and ritual of these sacrifices is described in Leviticus 1:3-4; 14:20; Ezekiel

43:19-27; 44:27; 45:17-23; and in Exodus 29:16; Leviticus 1:5, 11; 4:4-21, 25, 34.

While the burnt offerings are being made, the congregation stands in worship and the Levite musicians sing psalms and play *cymbals, harps, lyres,* and priests blow *trumpets.* They sing praises with gladness, a joyful assembly. The use of the instruments in worship and the singing of psalms by the Levites are attributed to *David,* the *prophets Gad* and *Nathan,* and the musician *Asaph,* of David's time.

Thank-offerings (described in Leviticus 7:12-17) are given in thanks for the renewal of worship in the Temple. The worshipers eat this offering as a festive meal. They eat nothing, however, of the animals offered for *burnt offerings,* which they bring with a willing heart, an essential element of true piety. The *consecrated offerings* are the sacrifices mentioned in verse 31. *The peace offerings* are the thank offerings. The *libations* (NRSV; NIV = *drink offerings*) are wine poured out like blood. The Chronicler is always a defender of the Levites over against the priests. The atmosphere is one of general rejoicing at the sudden turn from apostasy.

Invitation to All Israel to Return (30:1-12)

The king invites all Israel (verse 6). *Ephraim* and *Manasseh* are the largest provinces. The Northern Kingdom has its own center of worship (1 Kings 12:32-33) but, to the Chronicler, the only true center is the Temple.

The feast of *Unleavened Bread* (verse 13) is associated with the Passover, which normally occurs on the fourteenth day of the first month. The law (Numbers 9:9-12) permitted a postponement of the Passover to *the second month* (verse 3). *Beersheba to Dan* indicates the extreme southern to northern tips of Judah-Israel. The message of Hezekiah is the theme of Chronicles: Return to God (verses 6, 8-9).

Only a few from three northern tribes (Zebulun is the farthest north) respond to Hezekiah's request.

The Unity of God's People (30:13-27)

The Passover and the feast of Unleavened Bread are explained in Exodus 12:1-20; 13:6-10.

The Chronicler emphasizes the unity of God's people. A multitude from northern Israel (four tribes mentioned here) join those of Judah. Although considered ritually unclean, the northerners are treated kindly by Hezekiah, who prays for them. The Lord *healed* (pardoned) *them*. The zeal of the worshipers to remove the altars set up to foreign gods by Ahaz puts the priests and Levites to shame. The Chronicler speaks well of the lay Levites to whom *Hezekiah spoke encouragingly. Kidron valley*: See the note on 29:16. *Second month*: See the note on verse 2. The people worship, the Levites and priests make music, and the people eat the *peace offering* (thank offering).

This is an experience of great joy as in the time of Solomon (verse 26; see 7:8-9). The king and princes give generously (verse 24) and the priests increase in enthusiasm for the worship. *The whole assembly* (repeated three times) includes northern Israelites and *sojourners* (resident aliens).

Destruction of Pagan Religion (31:1)

The *high places and the altars* were set up to worship *the Asherim*, representations of a goddess supposed to preside over reproduction.

Contributions to the Temple Service (31:2-10)

The divisions of the priests and Levites are described and attributed to David and Solomon (1 Chronicles 23–27). The priests sacrifice at the altar. The ritual offerings are listed in Numbers 28–29. The Levites are gatekeepers and singers. *The camp of the* LORD (NRSV; NIV = *the* LORD's *dwelling*) is the Temple, figuratively the *tent of meeting* at the center of the pilgrim people, Israel (Numbers 2).

Hezekiah, like Solomon, supports the Temple service *from his own possessions* (2:4; 8:12-13). Verses 4-10 record the positive response of the people, not only those who live in Jerusalem but also all the people of Israel, to the command to bring the portions due to support priests and Levites. From *the third* month to the *seventh month* means from the first to the last harvest of the year. They bring in *heaps*, evidence of their religious devotion and the resulting prosperity with which God has blessed them.

Organization of the Priests and Levites (31:11-19)

Hezekiah arranges the storage of the *tithe* in Temple rooms and the distribution of the contributions. Levite officials are given separate responsibilities for storage and careful distribution of tithes for their support.

The priests come from their appointed cities to serve in the Temple according to their offices and to the time prescribed for their division (there being twenty-four divisions in all). They bring their families with them. *The descendants of Aaron* are the priests as distinguished from the other *Levites*. (For background see 1 Chronicles 23–27.)

Hezekiah's Service to the House of God (31:20-21)

These verses embody the Chronicler's ideal for the true Israel and its king.

The Threat from Assyria (32:1-23)

Similar accounts are in 2 Kings 16:9–19:37 and Isaiah 36–39. In 721 B.C. the Assyrian empire crushed Israel. Hezekiah's religious reform was a defiance of Assyria. Now the Assyrian power threatens Jerusalem. Hezekiah's faithfulness to the Temple and to God prepares the reader of Chronicles with the assurance that God will protect Hezekiah.

The Chronicler's sequence is not chronological but theological. Hezekiah relies on God but also takes vigorous action. As usual he consults his people, who give eager cooperation (verses 3-4; see 30:4, 23). He builds up the defenses, gathers arms, and organizes the army. His most famous act is the diversion of spring water into a tunnel (the Siloam Tunnel is still in use) within the fortified city. *The Millo* is the *fortified terraces* on Mount Zion at the lower eastern ridge of Jerusalem. Hezekiah states that God will not only help them, but will also fight their battles.

Boasting about the strength of their army and their god's might was typical of kings; it was an attempt to frighten the enemy into submission. Sennacherib has fought his way down through Philistia, threatening Judah's nearby *fortified cities. Lachish*, southwest of Judah, near Philistia, is one of the most strongly fortified cities in Judah. Sennacherib hopes Hezekiah will pay tribute to avoid destruction. The boast of Sennacherib reveals in summary the policy of Hezekiah: to centralize the religion of all Israel at the Temple of the Lord in Jerusalem. It also plays on the Chronicler's theme of reliance on God. There is a tendency, perhaps, to rely on Egypt, a reliance that Isaiah, the prophet, condemns (Isaiah 31:1-3).

Verses 17-19 express the Chronicler's outrage at the insult to God.

God's people are threatened. God's power is challenged. Prayer, reliance on God, is the only resource. The Chronicler has repeatedly affirmed this (13:14-16; 14:11-12; 20:1-19). *And the* LORD *sent an angel, who cut off.* According to Isaiah 37:36-37, it was by a plague.

Rest is a sign of God's blessing.

The Close of Hezekiah's Reign (32:24-33)

Except for the account of Hezekiah's sickness, the Chronicler makes much of the Solomon-like splendor of

Hezekiah, who comes nearer than any other king of Judah since Solomon to realizing the ideal kingdom that God intended for the chosen people.

The story of Hezekiah's sickness (for a fuller account see 2 Kings 20:1-11) reveals two of the Chronicler's truths: (1) When anyone in distress relies on God in prayer, God answers; and (2) pride turns God away; humbleness, which includes repentance, brings God's help. The *sign* is of the returning sun's shadow. It is described in 2 Kings 20:8-11.

The allusion to Hezekiah's fault and the postponement of God's wrath have to do with Hezekiah's indiscretion in showing all his treasure to the envoy of the king of Babylon, and the consequence: the Babylonian exile to come in later times (Isaiah 39:1-8).

Hezekiah's *very great riches and honor*, which archaeology corroborates, is evidence for the Chronicler that he is a second Solomon, approved by God.

The *Gihon* is a spring under the city of David, part of Jerusalem. Hezekiah diverts its waters (see verses 3-4). *Outlet* is the Hebrew word inscribed in Hezekiah's time on the tunnel wall. According to the Chronicler, the envoys from Babylon, interested in astrology, come to inquire about the sign of the changing shadow (verse 24). God leaves him to himself to test him.

The Chronicler closes his account of the reign of a devout king. He is buried *in the ascent of the tombs* (NRSV; NIV = *on the hill*), that is, in a place of honor.

§ § § § § § §

The Message of 2 Chronicles 29–32

The Chronicler uses the story of Hezekiah to portray the ideal religious society and to show how to achieve such a society. Although applied to Judah and Israel, this account has counsel for every believer in God:

§ to keep a clean and whole heart; to be faithful in the worship of God; to keep God's law and commandments; to seek God in all of life; to pray.

For every congregation:

§ to make the worship of God the priority and preference in life. Worship must always be consistent with loyalty to God, refusing every substitute for God, everything that would take away from the glorification of God.

§ to invite all to join in the worship of God, and to accept all and pray for the forgiveness of all fellow worshipers.

§ to worship in unity, wholeheartedly, using song and music to praise God, rejoicing together.

§ to bring tithes and offerings gladly for the support of those who are consecrated to the service of God.

For the people of God when threatened by disbelievers who would destroy their society of faith:

§ to be ready to defend the faith vigorously.

§ to trust in God courageously.

§ to ignore propaganda designed to weaken faith in God or to equate God with the gods and religions devised by the peoples of the earth.

§ neither to argue with nor to listen to propaganda that is designed to weaken faith in God.

§ § § § § § §

2 Chronicles 33–36

Introduction to These Chapters

These closing chapters of the Chronicles recapitulate, through the stories of the kings Manasseh and Josiah, the great goodness of faithfulness to God, the law, and the Temple, and the great evil of faithlessness to God, the law, and the Temple. The brief review of the last kings of Judah is like a descent into gloom, ending in tragedy, with a last faint glimmer of hope. The tragedy is that despite the promises of God, the ideal of the kingdom of David and Solomon, the messages from God through the prophets have not prevailed. In the end, the faithlessness of kings and people leads inevitably to doom. The last word, however, is that there will be yet another chance for restoration.

Here is an outline of these chapters.
I. Manasseh and Amon (33:1-25)
   A. Manasseh's seduction of Judah (33:1-9)
   B. Manasseh's humiliation and reform (33:10-17)
   C. The sum of Manasseh's life (33:18-20)
   D. Amon's short, evil reign (33:21-25)
II. Josiah's Faithfulness (34:1-33)
   A. Josiah's purging of Judah (34:1-13)
   B. The discovery of the Book of the Law (34:14-21)
   C. The judgment on Judah (34:22-28)
   D. The covenant made by Josiah (34:29-33)
III. Josiah's Celebration of the Passover (35:1-19)
IV. The Death of Josiah (35:20-27)
V. The Last of the Kings of Judah (36:1-21)

     A. Jehoahaz and Egypt (36:1-4)
     B. Jehoiakim, Jehoiachin, and Babylon (36:5-10)
     C. Zedekiah's and Judah's unfaithfulness (36:11-16)
     D. Destruction and exile of the people (36:17-21)
   VI. Cyrus of Persia: Hope for Jerusalem (36:22-23)

Manasseh's Seduction of Judah (33:1-9)

The abominable (NRSV; NIV = *detestable*) *practices* persist because they are easier than Hebrew faith, which requires worship of an unseen power who demands personal and social righteousness. People's immediate need is for a good crop yield, and good reproduction, human and animal. Pleasing the *Baals*, who own the soil, and the *Asherahs*, who command the life-forces, would avoid disease and ensure benefit. The sacrifice of children to fulfill vows was long practiced in such places as *Hinnom*, a deep valley below Jerusalem's walls (condemned by Jeremiah 19:5-6). *The host of heaven*, moreover, seem to give the Assyrians and Babylonians their great power. To worship them would ensure security (but see Deuteronomy 4:19; 17:3).

Manasseh's Humiliation and Reform (33:10-17)

Conforming to the world did not save Manasseh. God always warns against evil. But they who *gave no heed* faced disaster. There is no explanation as to why Manasseh is taken to Babylon. It foreshadows, however, the exile to Babylon of Judah's people, whose only hope is a return to the Lord. As always, in the Chronicles, in response to repentance God restores him. Verses 14-17 are typical of the Chronicler's report on good kings. The *Ophel*, a section of the City of David in Jerusalem, is above the spring of *Gihon*. *The Fish Gate* is in the north wall.

The Sum of Manasseh's Life (33:18-20)

Along with the note about his sin and faithlessness, the Chronicler adds the note about his prayer and his humbling himself. The Chronicler records neither honor nor dishonor for this king, who has a mixed record.

Amon's Short, Evil Reign (33:21-25)

Amon's evil is not cancelled by any sign of repentance. If the Chronicler's account of Manasseh's reforms were accurate and adequate, there would be no need of Josiah's reforms (34:1-7). Amon's apostasy, therefore, is used to suggest that all the altars and idols were restored by Amon.

Josiah's Purging of Judah (34:1-13)

When Josiah becomes king, the Assyrian empire is in decline, and Jeremiah, the prophet, is an influence in Judah.

The most positive phrase in the Chronicles is *seek God* (verse 3). This Josiah does from boyhood. At about age twenty he is secure enough to oppose popular religion. He destroys the platforms where sacrifices are made and where incense is burned to fertility gods. To the side of the platforms are representations of female fertility (*the Asherim*), and near or on the platforms are clay or metal images of fertility. His thoroughness includes the Samaritan north. The Chronicler claims the former Northern Kingdom of Israel, although now of mixed inhabitants, as still a part of God's Israel.

The Chronicler tells of Hezekiah's cleansing of the Temple from idolatry (29:15-19) and of Manasseh's influence (33:15-16). Josiah must now repair the Temple buildings. Money for the repair has been collected from much of old Israel as well as from Judah (see 24:4-14 where the collection is from Judah only). The work is under the charge of the king's financial secretary and the king's deputy prince of the city. The different Levitical offices are always in the Chronicler's mind in discussions about the Temple.

The Discovery of the Book of the Law (34:14-21)

The major event of Josiah's reign is the discovery of the Book of the Law. This book is believed to have been Deuteronomy 5–27. The book of Deuteronomy contains a warning: *If you will not . . . do all his commandments* (28:15), followed by awesome threats. To hear these would have been enough for King Josiah to have *rent his clothes*, a sign of great distress. He must find out what the Lord will do to those who are left *in Israel and in Judah*. The remnant of the Northern Kingdom is included.

The Judgment on Judah (34:22-28)

In the Chronicles, prophets come to warn kings for doing wrong. Here, however, the king, having read the general warning, seeks the prophet. *Huldah the prophetess* gives a double response. The doom foretold in the Book of the Law cannot be annulled because the people have turned against God. The Chronicler and his readers know that many things foretold in the law have happened and that more can happen unless they return to the law. The other response is to the king of Judah. God hears his prayers and will spare him the judgment on the people.

Huldah lives *in the second quarter* (NRSV; NIV = *district*) near the Temple where families of royal courtiers lived.

The Covenant Made by Josiah (34:29-33)

Many assemblies called by kings are recorded in the Chronicles. At this one, *the Book of the Covenant* is read aloud. *With all his heart* is the Chronicler's phrase for commitment.

Josiah's Celebration of the Passover (35:1-19)

This passage expands on 2 Kings 23:21-23. The Passover celebrates what it is to be an Israelite. It symbolizes the unity of all Israelites with God. Thus it becomes the fitting climax for Josiah's attempts to reform all Israel's religion (north and south). Like the account in chapter 30 of Hezekiah's Passover, this narrative may reflect the practice in the Chronicler's day. It includes his emphasis on the role of the Levites and the Temple. Sources for this celebration are Exodus 12:1-14 and Deuteronomy 16:1-8.

Evidently the priests need encouragement, so Josiah gives it to them. He also instructs the Levites. In the days when Israel wandered in the wilderness seeking a place to live, the Levites carried the ark in which the Ten Commandments were kept. Now, says Josiah, those days are past. The ark is in the Temple. The people must realize that the Levites have more important functions. They (and not just the priests) are the teachers of all Israel (17:7-9) and are *holy to the* LORD. *By your divisions* refers to the functions and schedules of service organized by David.

Often at great feasts the king gives away animals from his vast flocks. *His officials* also give generously. Chief priests and leading Levites supply the needs of priests and Levites. The lambs are for the Passover, and bulls are for peace offerings to accompany the great feast.

In this public celebration of the Passover, the ceremonial killing of the lamb, flaying it, and sprinkling its blood, are done by the priests and Levites on behalf of the people. In the first Passover, the blood of the lamb was sprinkled on the doorpost and lintel of each house (Exodus 12:7). In the public Temple ceremony, the priests sprinkle the blood on the altar. Parts of each offered lamb, like the bulls, are burned on the altar, then given to representatives of each extended family for them to present as a peace offering. *The singers* who accompany the service are descendants of those appointed by David: Asaph, Heman, and Jeduthun (1 Chronicles 15:16).

The feast of Unleavened Bread, celebrated to recall Israel's flight through the wilderness from Egypt, is associated with the Passover (Exodus 12:17-18; Deuteronomy 16:8). *No passover like it had been observed* (NIV;

NRSV = *kept* [see 30:26]). The distinct element in the Chronicler's account is the role played by the Levites, their value, their eager willingness, their unselfish service. *None of the kings of Israel* means all Israel, north and south inclusive.

The Death of Josiah (35:20-27)

This account parallels 2 Kings 23:29-30. Josiah's reign is one of new hope for Judah. His death fits the quick decline prophesied by Huldah (34:28). The historical setting is this: The Assyrian empire has fallen before a new empire based in Babylon. The fall of Assyria leaves a power vacuum that Egypt's pharaoh wishes to fill. He would use Judah and Israel as a buffer against the new power in the east. Josiah, thinking to preserve Judah's independence and authority over all of old Israel, challenges *Neco*. This is an annoyance to Neco, who defeats Josiah at Megiddo, the highway in the north of Israel. Neco goes on to fight, and be defeated by, the Chaldeans at Carchemish far to the north.

Neco's warning is interpreted by the Chronicler as a message from God, but Josiah *did not listen*. This explains his death (similar in details to that of Ahab in 18:29, 33-34) as a judgment. The honors shown the dead Josiah and the *laments* signify the Chronicler's evaluation of his goodness and faithfulness to God.

Jehoahaz and Egypt (36:1-4)

After Josiah's defeat, Judah is helpless before Neco of Egypt. *Jehoahaz* is Josiah's youngest son. (When Neco exiled him, Jeremiah wrote a dirge for him: Jeremiah 22:10-12.) The tribute figure, at a weight of 75 pounds per talent, is excessive.

Jehoiakim, Jehoiachin, and Babylon (36:5-10)

After Egypt's defeat at Carchemish, *Jehoiakim*, put on the throne by Egypt, transfers his allegiance to Babylon, the new power in the Middle East. He does what is evil, and is condemned (see Jeremiah 22:13-19). He rebels, although Jeremiah advises him not to (Jeremiah 27:9-11). Nebuchadnezzar besieges and captures Jerusalem.

Jehoiachin is eight years old (eighteen, according to 2 Kings 24:8) when he surrenders to Nebuchadnezzar. His exile, with most of the nobility, and the seizure of *precious vessels* are attributed to his evildoing.

Zedekiah's and Judah's Unfaithfulness (36:11-16)

His brother Zedekiah (verse 10) was actually *his uncle* (see 2 Kings 24:17), Josiah's third son (1 Chronicles 3:15). Nebuchadnezzar has made him swear allegiance, but under pressure from a pro-Egyptian party in Jerusalem, he rebels. Here is a typical triple pattern in Chronicles: (1) A king does wrong, (2) prophets warn him, (3) he humbles himself and is forgiven, or he does not humble himself (see 7:14).

Destruction and Exile of the People (36:17-21)

By forsaking God, the people have forfeited God's presence and protection. They refuse God's *compassion* (NRSV; NIV = *pity*) (verse 15), but the enemy has no compassion (verse 17). Not only do they take *the vessels of the house of God*, but they now burn the Temple. The people go into exile from the land God has given them.

Yet there is hope. There have been restorations in the past. The prophet Jeremiah had promised it in another seventy years (Jeremiah 25:11; 20:10-14). *Sabbaths* refers to years the land will have rest from work.

Cyrus of Persia: Hope for Jerusalem (36:22-23)

This added postscript repeats Ezra 1:1-3. Israel is God's people. Jerusalem is God's chosen city. The Temple is God's house. These have been the focus of the Chronicles. Now, through Cyrus, first emperor of the wide Persian empire, God will restore all three.

§ § § § § § §

The Message of 2 Chronicles 33–36

The theme of the books of Chronicles is repeated: God sends spokesmen to warn the people of wrong. If heeded, God will forgive and bless; if not and they forsake God, destruction is inevitable, and God's promise cannot be realized. The last kings slip back into evildoing so that the Temple and Jerusalem are destroyed, and the people exiled.

Chronicles uses history to:

§ warn against popular lifestyles that are really only a reversion to primitive paganism.

§ warn against all that opposes, or substitutes for, God.

§ assure that God has compassion for the people. That compassion, however, does not save them in spite of themselves. They must respond to God positively, not negatively.

§ assure that God judges and punishes those unfaithful to the law, but forgives those who humble themselves.

§ assure that to return to God means to seek God, worship God, and keep the law in total commitment.

§ remind us that God will not protect from harm those who do wrong and lead others away from God.

§ remind us that they who are faithful to God and deal justly are blessed by God and honored by people.

§ remind us that there is joy in community of praise to God.

§ counsel a pledge (covenant) with others to be faithful to God, to seriously keep the law and commandments.

§ counsel support of God's word and God's house.

§ counsel attention to those who speak for God.

§ counsel trust in and obedience to God despite social pressures and despite political expediency.

§ § § § § § §

Glossary of Terms

Abiathar: David's priest, deposed by Solomon.
Abijah: King of Judah, 919–914. Succeeded Rehoboam.
Adonijah: Son of David, hoped to succeed him as king.
Ahab: King of Israel, 869–850. He persuaded Jehoshaphat to join him in battle at Ramoth-gilead.
Ahaz: King of Judah, 735–715. Succeeded Jotham. Pressed by attacks from all neighbor nations.
Ahaziah: (1) King of Israel, 850–849. Succeeded Ahab. Engaged in venture in Arabia with Jehoshaphat. (2) King of Judah, 842. Succeeded Jehoram.
Ahijah: Inspired Jeroboam to be king of separated tribes of Israel.
Aijalon: A valley and town between Philistia and the hills of Judah and Benjamin.
Amalek: Nomadic tribe south of Judah. Conquered by David.
Amaziah: King of Judah, 800–783. Succeeded Joash. Defeated Edom. Defeated by Israel. Was assassinated.
Ammon: A nation near the Syrian desert, east of the Jordan River. At times controlled by Judah.
Amon: King of Judah, 642–640. Succeeded Manasseh. Under Assyrian control. Worshiped pagan gods.
Amorites: A people of Canaan, partly pushed east of Jordan by the Israelite invasion.
Asa: King of Judah, 913–873. Succeeded Abijah. Reformer. Waged war against Syria.

Asaph: Founder of a family of musicians; most famous of three or four musical guilds of psalmists.

Ashdod: A coastal city in northern Philistia.

Asherah: Goddess of fertility; mother goddess.

Athaliah: Queen of Judah 842–837. Widow of King Jehoram. Daughter of Ahab of Israel. Supported Baal worship.

Azariah: (1) Prophet who encouraged Asa in his reforms. (2) Slain son of King Jehoshaphat. (3) Army officer in the coup to overthrow Queen Athaliah. (4) High priest who rebuked King Uzziah.

Baasha: King of Israel, 900–877. Enemy of king Asa of Judah.

Bashan: Tableland east of the Sea of Galilee.

Ben-hadad: King of Damascus. Bribed by Asa to attack Israel.

Bethel: City on the boundary of Benjamin and northern Israel. (Made a sanctuary city of Jeroboam of Israel.)

Beth-horon: Fortified towns northwest of Jerusalem.

Beth-shemesh: A fortified city of Judah/Philistine border.

Carchemish: On the Upper Euphrates River near Asia Minor, where Neco of Egypt was defeated by Nebuchadnezzar in 605.

Chaldeans: A dynasty of kings who extended the Babylonian Empire over much of the Middle East, 626–539.

Cherethites: Part of King David's bodyguard.

Cyrus: Founder of Persian Empire. He allowed exiles to return to rebuild the Temple of Jerusalem, 538.

Dagon: Philistine god in whose temple the ark was placed.

Edom: A land and people southeast of Judah, south of Dead Sea; conquered by Judah, but later independent.

Elath or Eloth: Seaport at the head of the Gulf of Aqaba.

Eleazar: Ancestor of the high priests.

Eliezer: Prophet who rebuked Jehoshaphat for his joint trade venture with Israel on the Gulf of Aqaba.

En-gedi: An oasis on the west side of Dead Sea.

Ephod: A priestly garment. David's was a short kilt.

Ezion-geber: Port and foundry at head of Gulf of Aqaba.

Gath: Philistine city near the border of Judah.

Geba: City six miles northeast of Jerusalem.

Gedor: (1) City in southern Judah. (2) City in Benjamin.

Gershom: Son of Moses. An ancestor of Levites.

Gezer: An old Canaanite city in northwestern Judah.

Gibeon: Benjaminite city, northwest of Jerusalem.

Gihon: A spring below the City of David. Hezekiah channeled its waters under Jerusalem.

Gilead: Land east of the Jordan River. Same area as Gad.

Gozan: City, district, and river far north of Israel.

Hagrites: Bedouin tribe living east of Gilead.

Hamath: Northern point of Israel in valley near Mt. Lebanon.

Hanani: Prophet who rebuked Asa for not relying on God.

Hananiah: Family of Levite singers.

Hazael: Usurper of the throne of Damascus. He menaced King Joash of Judah.

Hazazon-tamar: Same as En-gedi.

Hebron: City of southern Judah. David's first capital.

Heman: Founder of a family or guild of Levite singers.

Hezekiah: King of Judah, 715–687. Succeeded Ahaz. Reformer. Revived worship at the Temple. Dug a tunnel for water into Jerusalem. Strengthened defenses. Attempted reconciliation with north Israelites.

Hilkiah: High priest in the reign of Josiah who supported the king's reforms and found the Book of the Law.

Hinnom: A deep valley below the south wall of Jerusalem, used at times for pagan worship and child-sacrifices.

Hittites: Non-Israelite people from north of Israel.

Huram (Hiram): King of Tyre who furnished Solomon with materials and craftsmen for building the Temple.

Iddo: Prophet in the time of Solomon and Rehoboam.

Ijon: Important city north of Israel captured by Assyria.

Ishbosheth: Son of King Saul who for two years tried to rule.

Ishmaiah: One of David's early comrades-in-arms.

Ithamar: Ancestor of lesser priests at the Temple.

Jabez: (1) Figure in an old folk story of Judah. (2) Place in Judah near Bethlehem.

Jachin: A priest and family of priests in Jerusalem.

Jebusites: The people from whom David captured Jerusalem.

Jeduthun: Founder and family of Levite singers, musicians.

Jehoahaz: (1) Ahaziah, king of Judah, 842. Succeeded Joram. (2) King of Judah, 609–608. Succeeded Josiah. He was carried into captivity in Egypt by Neco, king of Egypt.

Jehoiachin: King of Judah, 598–597. Succeeded Jehoiakim. He was carried into exile by Nebuchadnezzar, Babylon.

Jehoiada: High priest who overthrew Queen Athaliah (842–837) and Baal-worship. He enthroned Joash as king.

Jehoiakim: King of Judah, 609–598. Succeeded Jehoahaz.

Jehoshaphat: King of Judah, 873–849. Succeeded Asa. Allied with Israel, fortified Judah, organized army, set up educational program, judicial courts, commerce.

Jehu: (1) Prophet who rebuked Jehoshaphat for his alliance with Israel. (2) King who usurped Israel's throne, 842.

Jeroboam: First king of northern Israel, 922–901.

Jezreel: Town and valley, west of Jordan River.

Joash: King of Judah, 837–800. Succeeded Athaliah. Repaired the Temple, improved revenues, later broke with the priesthood. Avoided war by sending tribute to Hazael of Damascus. He was assassinated.

Joram: Jehoram, king of Judah, 849–842. Succeeded Jehoshaphat. Suffered from revolts and from neighbor nations.

Josiah: King of Judah, 640–609. Reformer. Repaired

Temple. Renewed and centralized worship for Judah and Israel in Jerusalem. Exercised some control over Samaria. Killed in battle with Egypt's King Neco at Megiddo.

Jotham: Regent (750–742) and king (742–735) of Judah. Succeeded Uzziah. Strengthened Judah's economy and army.

Kidron: Valley between Jerusalem and Mount of Olives.

Kiriath-jearim: Town eight miles north of Jerusalem. The ark of the covenant was kept here in early times.

Lachish: Fortified town on Judah's western border.

Maacah: Granddaughter of David's son, Absalom, wife of Rehoboam, mother of Abijah, worshiper of Asherah.

Manasseh: (1) Elder son of Joseph. A large tribe of Israel; settled both sides of the Jordan. (2) King of Judah, 687–642. Succeeded Hezekiah. Extended pagan religion, taken prisoner, according to Chronicles, to Babylon, and when released reverted to the worship of God.

Megiddo: Important city commanding Plain of Esdraelon in northern Israel. Josiah killed here in battle.

Merari: Ancestor of one of three branches of Levites.

Meunim, Meunites: Arab tribe from near Ma'an, southeast of Edom. Raiders in Judah where some remained.

Midian: A nomadic people east of the Gulf of Aqaba.

Moab, Moabites: Land and people east of the Dead Sea.

Mount Gilboa: Heights above the valley of Jezreel. Here Saul died after defeat by Philistines.

Mount Moriah: Rocky hilltop in Jerusalem. Site of Solomon's Temple, and today of the Mosque of Omar.

Nebuchadnezzar: King of Babylon, 605–562. He defeated the Egyptians in 605; captured Jerusalem, 597; destroyed it and the Temple, exiling the people, 586.

Neco: King of Egypt, 609–594. He killed Josiah in battle and installed Jehoiakim in his place, 609.

Negeb: Dry land south of Judah's hill country.

Obed-edom: (1) A citizen of Gath at whose house the ark rested. (2) A Levite guard at the Temple, son of Jeduthun, leading singer. (3) Levite musician.

Ophir: A land associated with the export of fine gold and algum wood. Located somewhere on the Red Sea coast.

Ornan: A Jerusalem Jebusite whose threshing floor on Moriah was bought by David to make a sacrifice to God. This became the site of Solomon's Temple.

Parvaim: Fine gold, probably from southwestern Arabia.

Pekah: Last king of Israel, 737–732.

Pelethites: Part of David's bodyguard.

Philistines: People living in the coastal plains west of Judah. They came about a century after the Israelites.

Pul: The name in Babylon for Assyrian king, Tiglath-pileser.

Ramoth-gilead: Frontier fortress east of Gilead, fought over by Israel and Syria. Ahab was killed fighting for it.

Rehoboam: King of Judah, 922–915. Succeeded Solomon after division of his kingdom. Threatened by Egypt, he built a string of fortresses. He supported pagan worship.

Seer: Originally, one who read omens and advised kings. Later identified as prophets who spoke for God.

Seir: Mountain range south of the Dead Sea. Homeland of Edom.

Sennacherib: King of Assyria and Babylonia, 705–681. He defeated Egypt, took tribute from Hezekiah. When challenged, he besieged Jerusalem, then left suddenly.

Shaphan: King Josiah's secretary. He helped in the great reform of Judah.

Sharon: Rich coastal plain west of Israel.

Shavsha: David's secretary in charge of legal documents.

Sheba, Queen of: Sheba was a tribe whose branch in south Arabia was active in overland trade in gold, spices, and other luxuries. The queen came to Jerusalem for trade talks with Solomon.

Shekel: About a half-pound weight in gold or silver.

Shemaiah: Prophet who forbade King Rehoboam to fight the seceding northern tribes of Israel.

Shephelah: Fertile foothills and valleys between Judah's hill country and the Philistine coastal plain.

Shishak: Libyan king of lower Egypt, 940–915. He invaded Judah and plundered Jerusalem in reign of Rehoboam.

Sojourners: Non-Israelites, both alien residents and descendants of inhabitants of the land before Israel.

Solomon: Third king of Israel (including Judah), 962–922. Succeeded David, built the Temple, prospered, developed commerce and military strength; famed for his wisdom.

Syria: Nation centered in Damascus, as is modern Syria. Enemy of Israel. Later allied with Israel against Judah. Bulwark against Assyrian power, it fell to Assyria in 732.

Tarshish: An important port on the Mediterranean. Its name was applied to large sailing vessels.

Tekoa: An important stronghold in the high hills of Judah.

Tiglath-pileser (Tilgath-pilneser): King of Assyria, 745–727. Ahaz of Judah appealed for his help, came under his control.

Uzziah: King of Judah, 784–742. Succeeded Amaziah. Under him agriculture and commerce prospered. He had military control of Philistia and Edom. He contracted leprosy.

Zadok: One of David's two priests and Solomon's only chief priest. His descendants retained the high priesthood.

Zechariah: Son of priest Jehoiada. He condemned the people for forsaking the Lord. Joash had him stoned.

Zedekiah: (1) Prophet who approved Ahab's plans and challenged and struck Micaiah for disapproving of them. (2) Last king of Judah, 597–587, succeeded Jehoiachin. In his reign, Judah, torn by rival parties, rebelled against Babylon, whose army then destroyed Jerusalem.

Zerah: An Ethiopian or Cushite leader who attacked Judah and was defeated by King Asa.

Ziklag: David's headquarters in southern Judah before he became king.

Zobah: Town and district north of Israel near Lebanon.

1 AND 2 CHRONICLES

Guide to Pronunciation

Abelmaim: AH-bel-MAH-yim
Abiathar: Ah-bee-AH-thar
Abijah: Ah-BEE-jah
Abishai: AA-bih-shigh
Achar: Ah-KAHR
Achish: Ah-KEESH
Ahaziah: Ah-hah-ZIGH-ah
Ahijah: Ah-HEE-jah
Ahimelech: Ah-HIH-meh-leck
Ahithophel: Ah-HEETH-oh-fel
Aijalon: AY-jeh-lon
Amalek: AM-ah-lek
Amariah: Am-ah-RIGH-ah
Aram-maacah: AR-am-mah-ah-CAH
Asaph: AY-saf
Asherah: Ah-sheh-RAH
Ashtaroth: AHSH-tah-roth
Athaliah: Ah-thah-LIGH-ah
Azariah: Ah-zah-RIGH-ah
Azekah: Ah-zeh-KAH
Azubah: Ah-ZOO-bah
Baal: Bah-AHL
Baasha: Bah-ah-SHAH
Bashan: Bah-SHAHN
Ben-hadad: Ben-hah-DAHD
Benaiah: Beh-NIGH-ah

Beracah: Ber-ah-CAH
Beth-horon: Beth-HOR-on
Beth-shemesh: Beth-SHEH-mesh
Bilhah: BIL-hah
Bezalel: BEZ-ah-lel
Carchemish: KAHR-keh-mish
Chaldeans: Kal-DEE-ans
Cherethites: KER-eh-thights
Cherubim: CHER-eh-bim
Eleazar: Eh-lee-AY-zar
Eliezer: Eh-lee-AY-zer
Eliphaz: EH-lih-faz
En-gedi: En-GEH-dee
Ephod: EE-fod
Ephraim: EE-frah-eem
Euphrates: You-FRAY-teez
Ezion-geber: EE-zee-on-GAY-ber
Geba: GAY-bah
Gedor: GAY-dor
Gezer: GEH-zer
Gihon: GEE-hon
Gozan: GOH-zan
Hamath: Hah-MAHTH
Hamath-zobah: Hah-MAHTH-ZOH-bah
Hanani: Hah-han-NEE
Hananiah: Hah-nah-NIGH-ah
Hazael: Hah-zah-ELL
Hazazon-tamar: HAH-zah-zon-TAY-mar
Hebron: Heh-BRON
Heman: Hay-MAHN
Hezekiah: Heh-zeh-KIGH-ah
Hilkiah: Hil-KIGH-ah
Hinnom: Hih-NOME
Hittites: HIH-tights
Hivites: HIH-vights
Horeb: HOR-eb
Huram: HYUR-am

1 AND 2 CHRONICLES

Ijon: IGH-jon
Ishbosheth: ISH-boh-sheth
Ishmael: ISH-mah-el
Ishmaiah: Ish-MIGH-ah
Issachar: IZ-zah-car
Ithamar: ITH-ah-mar
Jabez: JAH-bez
Jachin: Jah-KEEN
Japheth: JAH-feth
Jashobeam: Jah-SHOH-bih-em
Jebusites: JEB-you-sights
Jeconiah: Jeh-coh-NIGH-ah
Jeduthun: Jeh-DOO-thun
Jehiel: Jeh-HEE-el
Jehoahaz: Jeh-HOH-ah-haz
Jehoiachin: Jeh-HOY-ah-kin
Jehoiada: Jeh-HOY-ah-dah
Jehoiakim: Jeh-HOY-ah-kim
Jehoram: Jeh-HOR-am
Jehoshabeath: Jeh-hoh-shah-BEE-ath
Jehoshaphat: Jeh-HOH-sheh-fat
Jehu: JAY-hoo
Jerahmeel: Jeh-RAH-mih-el
Jerimoth: JER-ih-mothe
Jerioth: JER-ih-othe
Jeroboam: JER-oh-BOH-am
Jezreel: Jez-REEL
Joab: JOH-ab
Joash: JOH-ash
Josiah: Joh-SIGH-ah
Jotham: JAH-tham
Jushab-hesed: JOO-shab-HEH-sed
Kenizzites: KEN-ih-zights
Kidron: KID-ron
Kiriath-jearim: KIR-ee-ath-jeh-ah-REEM
Kohath: KOH-hath
Korah: KOR-ah

Kue: KOO-eh
Lachish: Lah-KEESH
Libnah: LIB-nah
Maacah: Mah-ah-KAH
Mahalath: Mah-hah-LAHTH
Manasseh: Muh-NASS-eh
Mareshah: MAH-reh-shah
Megiddo: Meh-GID-oh
Mephibosheth: Meh-FIB-oh-sheth
Merari: Meh-RAH-ree
Meshullam: Meh-SHOO-lam
Meunites: Meh-OO-nights
Micaiah: Mih-KIGH-ah
Midian: MIH-dee-an
Moab: MOH-ab
Moriah: Moh-RIGH-ah
Nahash: NAY-hash
Naphtali: Naf-TAL-lee
Nebuchadnezzar: NEB-oo-cad-NEZ-er
Neco: NEH-koh
Negeb: NEH-geb
Obed-edom: OH-bed-EE-dom
Ohel: OH-hel
Ophir: OH-fir
Parvaim: Par-VAY-im
Pekah: PEH-kah
Pelethites: PEL-eh-thights
Perez: PEH-rez
Philistines: FIH-liss-teens
Ramoth-gilead: Rah-mothe-GIH-lee-ad
Rehoboam: Ray-oh-BOH-am
Rephaim: Reh-fah-EEM
Seir: Seh-EER
Sennacherib: Seh-NAK-er-ib
Shammah: SHAH-mah
Shaphan: SHAY-fan
Shavsha: SHAV-shah

Shekel: SHEK-el
Shemaiah: Sheh-MIGH-ah
Shephelah: Sheh-FAY-lah
Shishak: SHEE-shak
Siloam: Sih-LOH-am
Simeon: SIH-mee-on
Sukkim: Soo-KEEM
Tadmor: TAD-mor
Tarshish: TAR-sheesh
Tekoa: Teh-KOH-ah
Tilgath-pilneser: TIL-gath-pil-NEE-zer
Tobadonijah: Toh-bad-oh-NIGH-jah
Tobija: Toh-BEE-jah
Uzzah: OO-zah
Uzziah: Oo-ZIGH-ah
Zadok: ZAY-dok
Zebediah: Zeh-beh-DIGH-ah
Zebulun: ZEB-you-lun
Zechariah: Zeh-kah-RIGH-ah
Zedekiah: Zeh-deh-KIGH-ah
Zemaraim: Zeh-mah-RIGH-im
Zephathah: Zeph-ah-THAH
Zerah: ZEH-rah
Ziklag: ZIK-lag
Zobah: ZOH-bah

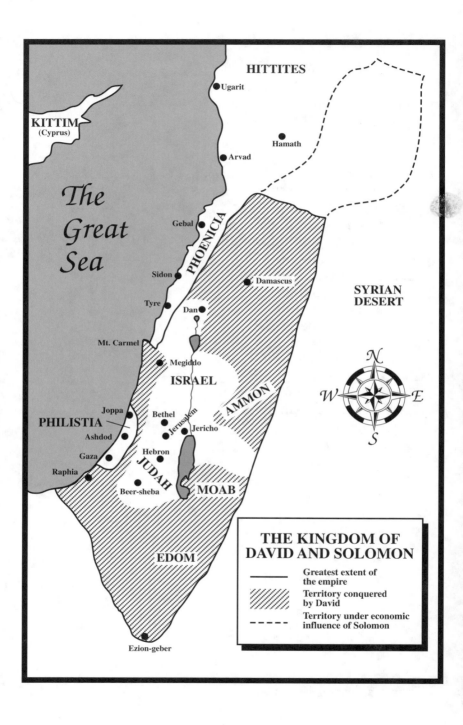

KITTIM
(Cyprus)

The Great Sea

HITTITES

●Ugarit

●Hamath

●Arvad

Gebal●

PHOENICIA

Sidon●

Tyre●

Dan●

●Damascus

SYRIAN DESERT

Mt. Carmel

Megiddo●

ISRAEL

AMMON

Joppa●

Bethel●

●Jerusalem

Jericho●

PHILISTIA

Ashdod●

Gaza●

Hebron●

JUDAH

Raphia●

Beer-sheba●

MOAB

EDOM

Ezion-geber●

THE KINGDOM OF DAVID AND SOLOMON

— Greatest extent of the empire

▨ Territory conquered by David

--- Territory under economic influence of Solomon

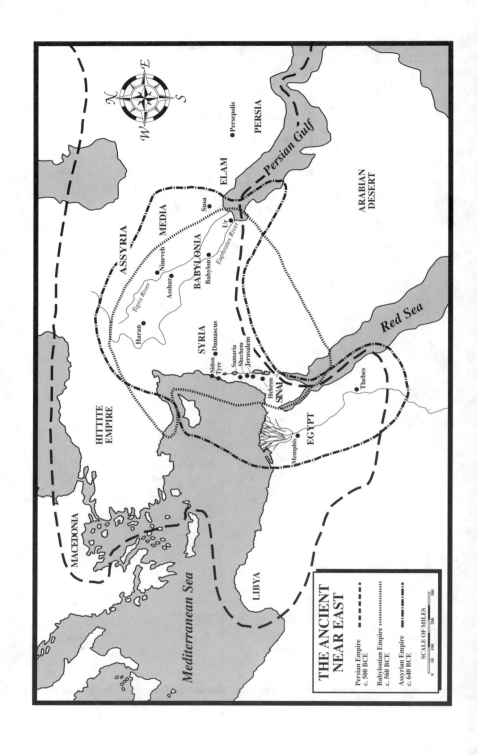

THE ANCIENT
NEAR EAST

Persian Empire
c. 500 BCE

Babylonian Empire
c. 560 BCE

Assyrian Empire
c. 640 BCE

SCALE OF MILES

0   50   100   200   300